AIRCRAFT OF THE ACES

128

ACES OF *JAGDGESCHWADER Nr* III

SERIES EDITOR TONY HOLMES

128

**AIRCRAFT OF
THE ACES**

Greg VanWyngarden

ACES OF *JAGDGESCHWADER* Nr III

OSPREY
PUBLISHING

First published in Great Britain in 2016 by Osprey Publishing

PO Box 883, Oxford, OX1 9PL, UK

PO Box 3985, New York, NY 10185-3985, USA

E-mail: info@ospreypublishing.com

Osprey Publishing, part of Bloomsbury Publishing Plc

© 2016 Osprey Publishing Limited

A CIP catalogue record for this book is available from the British Library

ISBN: 978 1 4728 0843 1

PDF e-book ISBN: 978 1 4728 0844 8

e-Pub ISBN: 978 1 4728 0845 5

Edited by Tony Holmes

Cover Artwork by Mark Postlethwaite

Aircraft Profiles by Harry Demspey

Index by Zoe Ross

Originated by PDQ Digital Media Solutions, UK

Printed in China through World Print Limited

16 17 18 19 20   10 9 8 7 6 5 4 3 2 1

Osprey Publishing supports the Woodland Trust, the UK's leading woodland conservation charity. Between 2014 and 2018 our donations will be spent on their Centenary Woods project in the UK.

www.ospreypublishing.com

Acknowledgements

The author owes a great debt to Adam Wait and O'Brien Browne for providing superb translations of German material. Dieter H M Gröschel, MD, shared valuable informa-tion from his studies. Grateful thanks are extended to historian Manfred Thiemeyer for his valuable photographs and information. Photographs were also provided by Rainer Absmeier, Lance Bronnenkant, Jörn Leckscheid and C J Bobrow. Researcher Bruno Schmäling also supplied important material and rare photographs. The assis-tance of Reinhard Zankl, Ray Rimell, Alan Toelle and Reinhard Kastner is greatly appreciated. The author would be remiss if he failed to acknowledge the contributions of his late friends Rick Duiven, Alex Imrie, Dan-San Abbott, Peter Grosz, George Williams, Neal O'Connor and A E Ferko. The writer's colleagues at *Over the Front* (www.overthefront.com), *Cross and Cockade International* (www.crossandcockade. com), and the Aerodrome Forum (www.theaerodrome.com) were also of great help.

Front Cover

In the early morning of 4 September 1918, 12 Sopwith Camels – two flights – from No 70 Sqn were heading deep into German territory near Douai, in northern France. The formation was led by Canadian Flight Leader Capt J H Forman DFC, a highly experienced ace with nine victories. At 3000 metres over Hamel, the RAF pilots sighted a group of seven Fokker D VIIs from *Jasta* 57 below them, led by their commander, Ltn d R Paul Strähle. One of the Camels dived to attack a straggling D VII, as Strähle subsequently recalled. 'One of our aircraft was lagging behind, and I turned around to aid him. It developed into an air fight, and since our *Staffel* was numerically [inferior] to that of the enemy, the air fight was not successful'. Indeed, two of the *Jasta* 57 Fokkers were shot up and one pilot was badly wounded in the stomach.

Fortunately, just in time, '*Jagdgeschwader Nr* III dropped down and joined in the attack', Strähle continued. 'They had more success. One Sopwith went down on fire'. The pilots from *Jastas* 26 and 27 of JG III were led by the *Geschwader* commander Oblt Bruno Loerzer, a celebrated 'Blue Max' winner with 37 victories. Loerzer flew a flamboyantly decorated Fokker that displayed the black and white stripes of *Jasta* 26 on its fuselage and tail – as the commander's machine it had the vivid striping extended to the wings too.

The veteran pilots of JG III, many of whom were flying the superb BMW-engined D VII, dropped out of the clouds from 3500 metres and savaged the Camel formation. As *Jasta* 27 ace Friedrich Noltenius wrote, 'A lively aerial battle with a strong Sopwith squadron commenced'. The 20-minute battle began at 0910 hrs, with the *Jasta* 26 Fokkers proving especially effective. Loerzer himself fastened on to one of the Camels and shot it down near Monchecourt for his 38th victory, while his adjutant, Oblt Theodor Dahlmann, was credited with a brace of British aircraft downed in two minutes over Palluel. *Jasta* 26's deadly Otto Fruhner brought his own tally to 23 by claiming three Camels, and his fellow ace Erich Buder added two more. Of the 12 Camel pilots from No 70 Sqn that originally engaged *Jasta* 57, only four made it back to their airfield.

CONTENTS

CHAPTER ONE

ORIGINS AND BACKGROUND

Royal Prussian *Jagdgeschwader Nr* III was the last of the trio of celebrated fighter wings of the German Army Air Service that achieved great success in aerial combat during the final year of World War 1. A *Jagdgeschwader* was a permanent grouping of four fighter squadrons (*Jagdstaffeln*, each with an official strength of 14 aircraft) under a permanent *Kommandeur*. It operated directly under the orders of the headquarters of the Army to which it was assigned. The first *Geschwader*, created on 23 June 1917, was the legendary JG I composed of *Jastas* 4, 6, 10 and 11 and commanded by Manfred *Freiherr* von Richthofen. Under his leadership and example, JG I compiled an enviable record and was referred to as the 'Richthofen Circus' by its British and American opponents.

The success of JG I led to the creation of two more such elite formations, designated JG II and JG III, on 2 February 1918. In addition, there was a fourth army *Jagdgeschwader* – the Royal Bavarian JG IV – and the Royal Prussian *Marine Jagdgeschwader,* but these units were formed very late in the war and had little opportunity for achievements comparable to those of JGs I, II and III.

JGs II and III were formed in preparation for the role the Air Service would play in the massive offensive that German forces were scheduled to launch on 21 March 1918. There would be three attacking German Armies in the assault (the 2nd, 17th and 18th), and the Air Service planned to

A view of Albatros D V 2329/17, heading a line-up of fighters that are all marked in the distinctive black and white colours of *Jasta* 26 at Iseghem in the late summer of 1917 *(courtesy R Absmeier)*

Title Page Spread
Two yellow-nosed Fokker Dr I triplanes and one new Fokker D VII of *Jasta* 27 are seen on the airfield at Halluin-Ost in this official *Kogenluft* photo taken in May 1918. The Dr I in the foreground displays some form of personal insignia that involves five-pointed stars, barely visible ahead of the fuselage cross

provide each of them with its own *Jagdgeschwader*, along with several more *Jastas* and many other air units. JG I would go to the 2nd Army, while JG II (*Jastas* 12, 13, 15 and 19) would go to the 18th Army. JG III was to be assigned to the 17th Army, and it would be comprised of the celebrated *Jasta* 'Boelcke' (formerly designated *Jasta* 2, but renamed *Jasta* 'Boelcke' after its first commander) as well *Jastas* 26, 27 and 36. That formation and its most successful pilots form the topics of this book.

A *Jagdgeschwader* was preferably led by a regular army officer who was not only a proven combat leader but also a successful air fighter. Suitably qualified officers were scarce, but JG III was fortunate to be led by Oberleutnant (later Hauptmann) Bruno Loerzer, one-time commander of *Jasta* 26 and already a prominent ace with nearly 20 victories. While JGs I and II both transitioned through three successive leaders due to combat deaths and injuries, JG III would serve throughout its entire nine-month career under Loerzer's leadership.

The reputation of Loerzer and his unit extended to the other side of the lines, as evidenced in American ace 'Eddie' Rickenbacker's book *Fighting the Flying Circus*. In writing of the opposition faced by his 94th Aero Squadron in October 1918, Rickenbacker recorded his belief that, 'The enemy had here concentrated the heaviest air force against the Americans that had ever been gathered together. Both the von Richthofen Circus and the Loerzer Circus were now opposed to us'.

By the time JG III was formed in February 1918 each of its four *Staffeln* had already been fighting at the front for months, compiling admirable records. It is appropriate to present brief summaries of their histories here so as to provide background knowledge and context for their accomplishments in the 'Loerzer Circus' in 1918.

JASTA 'BOELCKE'

Jasta 'Boelcke' was one of the most respected *Staffeln* at the front, ranking second only to von Richthofen's *Jasta* 11 in its number of victories. It had originally been formed as *Jasta* 2 under the leadership of Hptm Oswald Boelcke at Bertincourt on 27 August 1916. Boelcke was a legendary and charismatic figure to both the flying service and the German public, truly the father of German fighter aviation. Boelcke and his contemporary Max Immelmann were the first Fokker Eindecker aces and the first aviation recipients of the *Orden Pour le Mérite* (the highest Prussian award for bravery in combat, popularly known as the 'Blue Max'). The story of Boelcke and his famous command has been told many times (see *Osprey Aircraft of the Aces 73 – Early German Aces of World War 1* and *Osprey Aviation Elite Units 26 – Jagdstaffel 2 'Boelcke'*), so only a succinct account follows.

Boelcke's early group of handpicked pilots included future standouts Max Müller, Erwin Böhme and Manfred von Richthofen. Equipped with the Albatros D I and D II, these pilots announced their presence on the Somme front in spectacular fashion on 17 September when *Jasta* 2 destroyed four British aircraft – including Boelcke's 27th victory and the first of 80 for von Richthofen. Success followed success, with the *Staffel* tallying more than 50 victories by 26 October. Two days later, however, Boelcke met his tragic end when his Albatros collided in mid-air with

Oblt Bruno Loerzer commanded *Jagdgeschwader Nr* III throughout its existence, and would finish the war as a Hauptmann with the *Pour le Mérite* and 44 victories to his name. The latter half of his tally was scored during his tenure as *Geschwader Kommandeur*. Here, he displays his 'Blue Max' and a captured British leather flying coat – a highly prized item

the aircraft of his friend Erwin Böhme. Boelcke died of a fractured skull sustained in the resulting crash landing, while Böhme was able to land safely. All of Germany mourned the loss of their hero, but the airmen of *Jasta* 2, now under the leadership of Oblt Stefan Kirmaier, continued to rack up victories above the Somme.

Kirmaier himself fell on 22 November, just one day after another promising pilot had joined the *Staffel* – a 19-year-old from Krefeld named Werner Voss. Kirmaier's replacement as CO arrived on 29 November in the person of Oblt Franz Josef Walz. From 17 December 1916 onward, the *Staffel* was honoured by Imperial decree to include Boelcke's name in its official designation (sometimes recorded as *Jasta* 'B').

It was the frequent fate of the 'Boelcke' *Staffel* to lose its most successful *Jagdflieger*, as they were often transferred out to command other units. Thus, von Richthofen departed in late January 1917 to take over *Jasta* 11. Böhme also left that month for a temporary rest, but several newcomers would more than make up for the absence of these veterans. Werner Voss had initiated his string with a double victory on 27 November 1916, and he would add eight more before the end of February 1917.

23 February saw the arrival of Fritz Otto Bernert from *Jasta* 4, with seven victories. March 1917 really belonged to Voss, who tallied 11 more successes and was awarded the *Pour le Mérite* on 8 April. Bernert was credited with 15 Royal Flying Corps (RFC) aircraft during April to bring his own total to 24. By the end of April 1917 the unit's total of victories stood at 139. Two of those had been achieved by Ltn d R Hermann Frommherz for his initial victories. A 26-year-old from Baden, he had served in *Kampfstaffel* 20 of *Kagohl* 4 alongside Werner Voss in 1916. Frommherz would eventually rise to great prominence and play a pivotal role in JG III.

Voss was transferred to *Jasta* 5 on 20 May 1917, while Walz left to take command of Bavarian *Jasta* 34 and was replaced by Otto Bernert. In the summer of 1917 the fortunes of *Jasta* 'B' suffered a downturn. Only one victory was scored in all of June, that being a Sopwith Pup downed by Ltn d R Friedrich 'Fritz' Kempf on the 5th. Like Frommherz, Kempf hailed from Baden, and his name, too, would feature in the story of JG III. July passed without a single victory, and only one came in August – a Sopwith Camel that went down on the 17th to Ltn d R Johannes Wintrath as his first *Luftsieg* (air victory). Born on 13 September 1893 in Dortmund, Wintrath had arrived in February after two-seater service in *Flieger-Abteilung (A)* 221. Wintrath went on to claim another Camel at 1735 hrs on the 19th, but that Sopwith was recorded as merely *zur Landung gezwungen* (*zLgw* – forced to land behind enemy lines) and was not added to Wintrath's tally.

Luckily for the *Staffel*, August also saw the return of the talented Paul Bäumer, who had previously served a mere two days in *Jasta* 'Boelcke' at the end of June before being posted to *Jasta* 5 for about six weeks. Bäumer was born on 11 May 1896 in Duisberg, and was seized by 'aviation fever' at a young age. Although a dental apprentice, he was taking flying lessons at Holten in August 1914. Indeed, just before Bäumer could take his examination for his aviator's certificate, the war broke out.

His attempts to enlist in the Air Service in the ensuing days were rejected, and he instead volunteered for service in *Infanterie-Regt Nr* 70

By the late summer of 1917 *Jasta* 'Boelcke' was equipped with the Albatros D V, including 1072/17 flown by Ltn d R Johannes Wintrath. It displays the unit's all-white tail marking, characteristic of this period. Wintrath's personal emblem was a blue-white-green diagonal band on the fuselage. Previously, it was thought that the fuselage was left in its factory finish, but this photo reveals that it was actually overpainted in a light colour, perhaps blue (*R Kastner*)

Paul Bäumer was one of the star turns of *Jasta* 'Boelcke'. Here, he poses with his Albatros D V 4409/17, which he flew for his sixth and seventh victories in the autumn of 1917. His personal edelweiss emblem was painted on a black band edged in red (*H-K W Dittman*)

at Saarbrücken. Bäumer saw action at St Quentin, on the Western Front, and then experienced considerable fighting on the Eastern Front. A wound sustained on 28 February 1915 resulted in travel to a hospital in Germany, where he reapplied to the Air Service and was accepted in August 1915. Bäumer underwent military flying training at *Flieger-Ersatz-Abteilung* (*FEA*) 1, an aviation replacement unit at Döberitz, and in October he was posted to *Armee-Flugpark* (*AFP*) 1 as an instructor and ferry pilot. Bäumer was promoted to Gefreiter on 19 February 1917 and on 26 March he was sent to *Flieger-Abteilung* (*FA*) 7, where he was soon promoted to Unteroffizier. On 15 May he was awarded both his Pilot's Badge and the Iron Cross 2nd Class for his work as a reconnaissance pilot. He also took the opportunity to take a captured British Nieuport aloft, which strengthened his desire to fly fighters. On 11 June Bäumer was posted to *AFP* 4 and then to the *Jastaschule* near Valenciennes.

As noted, Bäumer was sent to *Jasta* 5 at the beginning of July after two days at *Jasta* 'B'. He wasted little time, burning an observation balloon on 12 July, followed by two more gasbags on the 13th and 15th. He then returned to *Jasta* 'Boelcke' and continued piling up victories.

By then the *Jasta* command had passed to Erwin Böhme, and under his leadership the *Staffel* began to improve. Six more RFC aircraft fell to the unit in September in exchange for the loss of three pilots killed – including Wintrath. The unit racked up 11 victories in October, and Bäumer added nine of his own the following month. On 24 October the *Jasta* lost the services of Hermann Frommherz, who was posted to *FEA* 3 at Gotha, then to the flying school at Lübeck as an instructor. In mid-November 1917 the *Staffel* had moved to Bavichove in the 4th Army sector. By the end of November the *Staffel* tally had reached 180, but on the 29th day of that month Böhme was killed in action.

On 13 December 1917 the veteran ace Ltn Walter von Bülow-Bothkamp was brought in from *Jasta* 36 to take command of the *Staffel*. This highly experienced aristocrat was one of four brothers who served in World War 1 – the eldest, Friedrich, had already fallen in August 1914. The other three all became pilots in the Air Service. Of those three, Walter was the oldest, followed by Conrad. Harry, the youngest, would transfer to *Jasta* 'Boelcke' from *Staffel* 36 on 2 January 1918. By that time Walter had 28 victories and the *Pour le Mérite* and Harry had downed three opponents of his own. His name would later figure prominently in JG III.

As leader of *Jasta* 36, Walter had been invited to attend demonstrations of the new Fokker Dr I triplane at Adlershof in November 1917. It was intended to equip the elite *Geschwader* formations with the triplane, and Walter was told of the plans to form JG III in the 4th Army at this time. *Jasta* 'Boelcke' was likely the first unit to be earmarked for inclusion in JG III. On 1 January 1918 the *Jasta* received examples of the rotary-engined Fokker D V. The D V was primarily a trainer, used to help pilots transition from their stationary-engined Albatros fighters to rotary-engined machines in preparation for receiving triplanes. However, Walter von Bülow fell in combat on 6 January 1918 and *Jasta* 'Boelcke' was again leaderless.

Jasta 'B' began receiving Fokker Dr Is in early January 1918. Here, Ltn d R Paul Schröder (second from left) and his groundcrew pose with his triplane, 157/17. It has already been decorated with the *Staffel* marking of a half-white, half-black tail section. The black(?) and white stripes on the fuselage were Schröder's personal markings, and these stripes would later be added to the interplane struts as well

One of the last survivors of the original *Jasta* 2, Ltn d R Otto Höhne was posted in from *Jasta* 59 in late January to take over. However, Höhne soon realised he was not up to the task. 'He gave the leadership up again after a short period because he felt that he was not mature enough for the requirements', wrote Ltn Carl Bolle, his successor. Bolle, a veteran of service in *Jasta* 28, took over on 20 February 1918 just as JG III was forming. Bolle proved to be both a superb leader and fighter pilot, and he led *Jasta* 'B' in exemplary fashion for the rest of the war. By 10 January 1918 a number of the new Fokker Dr Is had arrived, and more were assigned to *Jasta* 'B' in the ensuing weeks.

On 3 February 1918, just as JG III was forming up, the *Jasta* 'Boelcke' pilots had a brilliant day with their new triplanes. At 1040 hrs Ltn d R Otto Löffler shot down DH 4 A7873 from No 25 Sqn at Mariakerke, near Ghent, for his second *Abschuss* (victory), both crewmen being wounded and taken prisoner. At 1510 hrs Ltn d R Paul Schröder achieved his sole victory by downing Camel B6430 from 9 Naval Squadron east of Moorslede, killing Acting Flt Cdr R R Winter. At the same time Ltn d R Hermann Vallendor also attained his first with an SE 5a. Both Löffler and Vallendor would play conspicuous roles in the annals of JG III. With successes such as these adding to the legacy of their famous unit, the men of *Jasta* 'Boelcke' prepared to move to Marcke to join the other units of JG III in the vicinity of Courtrai (Kortrijk, Belgium).

JASTA 26

Jagdstaffel 26 had been established at *FEA* 9 in Darmstadt on 14 December 1916 through *Kommandeur der Flieger* 9 (the *Kofl* was an officer in charge of all the aviation units within an Army). The logistics and effort involved in assembling the necessary men, aircraft and other equipment took about five weeks. On 18 January 1917 the unit was transported by train to its first airfield

This photo from the Hermann Göring albums depicts his own Albatros D III 2049/16 in its initial guise at *Jasta* 26. He first flew this machine on 24 February 1917, and would use it throughout 'Bloody April'. At first, like other D IIIs in *Staffel* 26, it bore only a personal marking of coloured bands on the clear-varnished fuselage – this was before the familiar unit markings of broad black and white bands were instituted for *Jasta* 26. Göring took this D III with him when he was transferred to command *Jasta* 27 in May, where it was painted over in its more familiar black fuselage and white nose and tail markings

Another photo from the Göring albums reveals a *Jasta* 26 Albatros D III having its engine replaced, circa April/May 1917. The famous black and white banded markings that came to identify *Jasta* 26 aircraft may have been applied in stages. There are several similar photos that show D IIIs from this time painted with only the black bands, with the rest of the fuselage left in its factory finish. Perhaps the photos captured the aircraft in a transitional period. The black bands were also applied to the camouflaged uppersurfaces of the tailplane

at Colmar Nord in Alsace, in the sector of *Armee-Abteilung* B. Its first commander was Oblt Bruno Loerzer, who remained associated with the unit for the rest of the war. Even after he left the *Staffel* to assume overall command of JG III, Loerzer would continue to fly with *Jasta* 26, and his personal aircraft continued to display the unit's distinctive black and white markings.

Loerzer was born in the Berlin suburb of Friedenau on 22 January 1891. He qualified as a *Fahnenjunker*, or officer candidate, in the 4th *Badisches Infanterie-Regt 'Prinz Wilhelm' Nr* 112, and obtained his commission on 27 January 1913. It was in this regiment that Loerzer met, and befriended, a certain Hermann Göring. The careers of the two friends were intertwined from then on (readers looking for a detailed account of Göring's World War 1 career should read Peter Kilduff's book *Hermann Göring – Fighter Ace)*. Loerzer experienced his first flight in the spring of 1914, and his resultant request for a transfer to the flying corps was granted – he was sent to the *Militär-Fliegerschule* located at Habsheim on 15 July 1914. When the war began, the school was moved to Freiburg, more distant from the front.

During his training in Freiburg Loerzer was reunited with Göring, who was recuperating from rheumatoid arthritis in the local hospital. Loerzer suggested that his friend also transfer to aviation to serve as his observer. Loerzer was soon ordered to *FEA* 3 at Darmstadt for advanced training, and Göring managed to join him there for observer's training. Upon completion of his schooling Loerzer was ordered to *Feldflieger-Abteilung* (*FFA*) 25 as a pilot, and once again Göring would join him there through a combination of guile and bluff. The two flew many missions together from their base at Stenay.

FFA 25 was part of the 5th Army under the nominal command of Crown Prince Wilhelm (eldest son of the Kaiser). The Loerzer/Göring team frequently made their reconnaissance reports directly to the Crown Prince and he befriended both of them, becoming something of a patron. As Loerzer later wrote, 'Over the course of time the Crown Prince became a sort of protector for us. Subsequently, when I became a fighter pilot and fought over other army sectors, he continued to be kept informed [of my activities]'. The support of this royal benefactor would be a great asset to both Loerzer and Göring throughout the war.

In July 1915 Göring left *FFA* 25 for pilot training, at the same time that Loerzer was attending

the Fokker single-seater school at Schwerin-Görries. The two eventually
returned to *FFA* 25, where, on 16 November, pilot Göring and his observer
would receive credit for downing a French Farman. In July Göring was
assigned to *Artillerie-Flieger-Abteilung* 203 to fly fighters, and Loerzer
soon followed him there. On 9 January 1916 Loerzer was posted to
Kampfeinsitzer Kommando (*KEK*), or single-seater detachment, 'Jametz'
to fly Fokker monoplanes. He soon scored his first two victories, but was
wounded on 3 April. Later, both Loerzer and Göring served brief tours in
Kampfstaffel 'Metz' before being posted to the new *Jasta* 5 in the 1st Army.
However, on 18 January 1917, Loerzer was assigned to form and lead
the new *Jasta* 26, where Göring joined him on 15 February. The *Staffel*
was equipped with new Albatros fighters, and Göring was assigned D III
2049/16, which he would fly for several months.

Another founding member of *Jasta* 26 was Bruno Loerzer's younger
brother Fritz. Born on 27 July 1893, Fritz was a theology student before the
war and was widely known as 'the flying pastor' in Air Service circles. He
received his training at *FEA* 2 in Adlershof, then *FEA* 1, before proceeding
to Schwerin-Görries for fighter training on 15 August 1915. He joined
his brother at *KEK* 'Jametz' on 12 March 1916, before being posted to
Jasta 6 in late August. After achieving his initial victory in that unit on
16 November, Vzfw Loerzer arrived at *Jasta* 26 on 14 February 1917 and
was soon flying patrols in Albatros D III 2024/16.

The honour of tallying the first
confirmed victory for *Jasta* 26 fell to Ltn d
R Weitz on 25 February when he downed
a French Nieuport. Bruno Loerzer added
the unit's second and third victories in early
March, and his brother Fritz was credited
with a Nieuport on 16 March for the fifth
success of the *Staffel*. One month after that,
Jasta 26 relocated to a field east of Guise
in the 6th Army sector on the Somme.
Now opposing the RFC and Royal Naval
Air Service (RNAS), the *Staffel* played its
part in 'Bloody April' by bringing down
five British machines – one of those fell to
Bruno Loerzer and three more to Göring.

This superb study of three *Jasta* 26
Albatros D IIIs shows two – including
2040/16 in the foreground – that have yet
to receive any new markings. At extreme
left is 2070/16, which displays the classic
Jasta 26 colour scheme of broad black/
white bands on its fuselage and horizontal
tail surfaces – the fin and rudder were not
yet painted black. Although this
identification is not certain, the pilot in
2040/16 resembles Fritz Loerzer, who is
also recorded as having flown 2024/16
(*L Bronnenkant*)

This *Jasta* 26 Albatros D V 1103/17 was
part of the initial production batch of D Vs,
numbered 1000/17 to 1199/17. These
first D Vs began arriving at the front in
May/June 1917, just as *Jasta* 26 was
transferred to Iseghem airfield. D V
1103/17 displays the unit's famous black/
white banded markings and a personal
W insignia

Examples of the second production batch of the Albatros D V began arriving at the front around September 1917. One of them was 2329/17, seen here resplendent in *Jasta* 26 livery. Although the pilot is unknown, his personal marking was the emblem of the German Gymnastics Association, made up of four Fs combined. These stood for the group's motto of *'Frisch, fromm, frölich, frei'* (vigorous, pious, cheerful, free)

By 17 May 1917, Göring's total of seven victories had earned him the command of *Jasta* 27 and he left Loerzer's *Staffel*.

On 8 June *Jasta* 26 was transferred from Bohain to Iseghem airfield in the 4th Army sector. July 1917 was to be the most successful month yet for the *Staffel*, with seven British opponents downed. Fritz Loerzer added two more RFC aircraft to his list in August – a month in which pilot Ltn d R Xaver Dannhuber scored his first four successes. Dannhuber, incidentally, was the pilot photographed with Albatros D V 2299/17 marked with a personal six-pointed star emblem – this was not Bruno Loerzer as has often been stated (as in *Osprey Aircraft of the Aces 32 – Albatros Aces of World War 1).* By this time the aeroplanes of the *Jasta* had been adorned with flamboyant unit markings of broad black and white bands around the fuselage and tail, as seen on Dannhuber's D V.

In September these distinctive fighters were becoming well known to the RFC airmen who encountered them. Two of the unit's September victories were achieved by Vzfw Otto Fruhner when he downed a brace of Camels on the 3rd for the first two of an eventual 27. Bruno Loerzer had increased his own score to 11 by the end of September. He was also kept busy in October, bringing his score to 20 by the 30th – one of his victims was No 56 Sqn ace Charles H Jeffs, who was taken prisoner on 5 October and entertained by the *Jasta* 26 airmen. Four days later Dannhuber seems to have downed Capt W Rooper, an eight-victory Nieuport pilot of No 1 Sqn. Other RFC pilots from the unit reported that their opponents were 'black and white Albatros Scouts'. By the end of October Loerzer's unit had been credited with more than 50 enemy aircraft.

Jasta 26 was earning a reputation as one of the best *Staffeln* in the 4th Army as it continued to engage the RFC from its base at Bavichove. On 8 November an SE 5a flight from No 56 Sqn attacked a formation of six 'black and white Albatri' over Moorslede – Lt Cobbold fell to the guns of Fritz Loerzer for his fifth victory. One week later Vzfw Otto Esswein knocked down a Camel from No 65 Sqn for the first of an eventual 12 victories. Esswein was from Württemberg, having been born on 3 March 1890 in Waiblingen. He had transferred to the Air Service in mid-1915, and following a stint at the *Jastaschule* he had arrived at *Jasta* 26 on 30 October. Esswein was lightly wounded on 27 November but remained at the front.

Bruno Loerzer's 20th victory on 30 October 1917 was followed by the award of the Royal Hohenzollern House Order (often known simply as 'the Hohenzollern') sometime in late 1917. This decoration was considered a customary predecessor to the award of the *Pour le Mérite*, and his 20th victory certainly put Loerzer in consideration for that order as well.

In December four victories were gained in exchange for one pilot injured in a crash and another shot down in flames. Fortunes improved in the first month of 1918, especially for Otto Fruhner. A native of Brieg, in Silesia, he was born on 6 September 1893. Fruhner began his career in the Air Service as a mechanic, being posted to *FEA* 4 in Posen on 20 November 1914. In early 1915 he was sent to the *FEA* at Graudenz and then to the flying school at Köslin. From May 1916 Fruhner served as a reconnaissance pilot with *FA* 51 on the Eastern Front. His good work in that unit, and in *FA* 20, brought promotion to unteroffizier in August.

In July 1917 Fruhner was detached from his unit to attend *Jastaschule* I, and then went to *Jasta* 26 on 11 August for the start of his eventful 14 months with the unit. On 3 January 1918 he was credited with a Sopwith for his third victory, followed by a two-seater the next day, which is generally credited as his fourth. Bruno Loerzer downed a Bristol F 2B Fighter from No 20 Sqn on 19 January – the same day he was ordered to attend the fighter aircraft type tests and competition in Berlin. Otto Fruhner was credited with Sopwiths on 22 and 29 January.

By late January 1918 the pilots of *Jasta* 26 were looking forward to re-equipping with the Fokker Dr I as part of JG III. Although the triplanes had not yet arrived, the pilots began their training on Fokker D Vs in preparation. On 2 February Esswein claimed a Camel for his second victory, and on the 3rd the Albatros pilots of the *Staffel* had an impressive day, with Esswein gaining credit for three Sopwiths and Fruhner two more. *Jasta* 26 was ready to begin its work in JG III with a record of more than 70 victories.

Jasta 26 members entertain an unwilling guest on 5 October 1917, as Oblt Bruno Loerzer (second from left) poses next to his 13th victim, Lt C H Jeffs of No 56 Sqn, who had been shot down in SE 5a B524. At extreme left in the back row, hand on hip, is Otto Fruhner. Fritz Loerzer is standing just behind Jeffs' right arm. To the right of Jeffs, with cigarette, is Ltn d R Xaver Dannhuber. The pilot at extreme right in the back row is Ltn d R Walter Blume, who would leave *Jasta* 26 after being wounded on 29 November. He would eventually command *Jasta* 9 and earn the *Pour le Mérite*, surviving the war with 28 victories (*L Bronnenkant*)

Jasta 26 pilots continued to fly the Albatros D V and D Va through the winter of 1917/18 and after the formation of JG III. In this blemished and undated photo, mechanics work on the engine of D V 2242/17. The pilot is unknown, but his personal insignia was the black(?) circle on the fuselage. On most *Jasta* 26 D Vs the military serial number on the fin was not obscured, being retained in a small unpainted rectangle

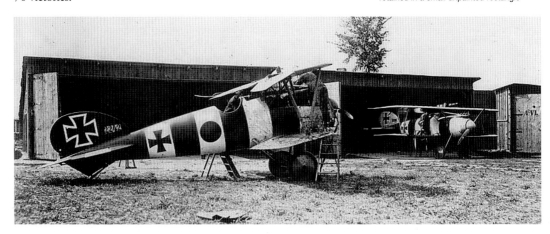

JASTA 27

On 5 February 1917 *Jagdstaffel* 27 was established through *Kofl* 9, with Ltn Hans von Keudell as its first CO. The latter was a veteran of *Jasta* 1 with 11 victories and a stellar reputation. The war diary of the new *Staffel* stated that;

'Two aircraft, with pilots and mechanics, are to be given up to *Jasta* 27 by both *Jastas* 8 and 18. In addition, three aircraft shall be supplied by *AFP* 4-Ghent, and the *Staffel* commander, with his own aircraft, will bring the total number of aircraft assigned to this new *Staffel* to eight.'

The first mobilisation day for *Jasta* 27 was 5 February 1917. Keudell took the unit to Ghistelles in the 4th Army sector in anticipation of the next Allied offensive. On 15 February he led a flight of three Albatros D IIIs over Boesinghe. Keudell attacked a Nieuport two-seater from No 46 Sqn, only to be shot down and killed – in spite of this, he was credited with 'downing' the Nieuport for his 12th victory, and the first for *Jasta* 27.

The unit's second CO was Ltn d R Phillip Wieland, who had managed to down a BE 2 while a member of *FFA* 6 and then served four months in *Jasta* 8, before arriving at *Jasta* 27 on 22 February. In late March 1917 the *Staffel* was transferred south to the 6th Army sector – from February to May the *Jasta* failed to add to its single victory, suffering three casualties during this period. When Ltn d R Helmut Dilthey arrived on 19 May, he complained of the unit's lack of potent machines;

'Our fighter aeroplanes were mostly technically inferior to those of the enemy. Speed and ceiling were too low. When I came from *FFA* 50 to *Jagdstaffel* 27, we had only three combat-ready aeroplanes there. Thus, with its technically inferior single-seaters at the time, the *Staffel* had no aerial victories at all. When we got Ltn Göring as *Staffelführer*, it became better, for not only did he already have seven aerial victories, he also pleaded our case very energetically to the higher-ups.'

The ambitious Göring was posted in on 17 May, and he soon put his talents for ingratiating himself with senior officers to good use. It seems he quickly got rid of most of the unit's inferior Roland aircraft and increased the inventory of Albatros D III and D V fighters. Indeed, Göring had brought his own D III 2049/16 with him from *Jasta* 26 and had it repainted with a black fuselage, white nose and tail. The Albatros types were at least comparable to the latest generation of Allied fighters, and with them the fortunes of the *Jasta* gradually improved. On 8 June Göring made his first contribution to his unit's score book by downing the Nieuport of Australian 2Lt F D Slee of No 1 Sqn, who was captured. In a typically bombastic account written in 1920, Göring claimed that Slee was 'an experienced fighter pilot, who had already shot down five German aeroplanes'. In reality, Slee was a neophyte on his first mission over the lines.

Soon after this, *Jasta* 27 was notified that the *Staffel* was to move from its base in Bersée, in France (6th Army sector) to Iseghem, in Belgium, (4th Army sector) in anticipation of what would become known as the Third Battle of Ypres. The *Staffel* had completed the move by 19 June, and Göring was now reunited with Loerzer and *Jasta* 26. Flying on the 'hot' Flanders front, *Jasta* 27 faced a new level of opposition. On 16 July Göring's flight tangled with SE 5as from No 56 Sqn, and both Göring and Vzfw Max Krauss received credit for victories (although No 56 Sqn suffered no casualties). Göring's favourite D III 2049/16 was disabled during the combat, prompting him to subsequently write 'the motor suddenly fell out and hung only loosely in the construction'. A photograph of the damaged Albatros suggests that the synchronisation gear of the guns malfunctioned and their fire shattered the propeller. Göring managed a crash landing but never flew 2049/16 again. He switched to D V 2080/17 and recorded his tenth victory on 24 July.

Seven days later the Third Battle of Ypres began, and in August *Jasta* 27 recorded eight machines downed for the loss of one pilot killed. In September Göring contributed two victories to a total of ten for *Jasta* 27 – two of those ten were also credited to a promising newcomer named Rudolf Klimke.

Although a fledgling single-seater pilot, Klimke came to the *Staffel* with a wealth of impressive flying experience. Born in Merseburg on 8 November 1890, he commenced military service with *Feldartillerie-Regt (FA) Nr* 75 in 1910 but went to war with *FA Regt Nr* 10. He transferred to the Air Service on 8 August 1915, and was posted to *FFA* 55 in 1916. For nearly a year Klimke and his observer, Oblt Leon, flew missions on the Eastern Front and were credited with downing a Russian aircraft on 25 September. Klimke and Leon were then transferred to *FA* 19 in Flanders in early 1917, under Hptm Baer.

Klimke had taught himself night flying during his Eastern Front service, and together with Leon he now made many night bombing raids deep into enemy lines. Soon, the pair began to consider the idea of flying to London, and received permission to undertake such a mission from Baer. They took off in their Albatros C VII on the moonlit night of 6/7 May and navigated their way to London successfully, Leon dropping five 10 kg bombs on the city. After a four-hour flight the two *Londonflieger* returned safely to be rewarded with a very raucous celebration (this was the first occasion any heavier-than-air craft had attacked London at night).

Shortly after this, Klimke and Leon were posted to *Staffel* 13 of *Kampfgeschwader* III, which was preparing for the famous Gotha daylight attacks on London. The pair (along with Vzfw Rientrop) flew their Gotha in the celebrated London raid of 7 July 1917, when they claimed a Sopwith shot down for Klimke's second victory. In spite of this success, Klimke and Leon disliked flying the cumbersome Gothas and returned to their old *FA* 19. After Leon became the CO of that unit, Klimke requested a transfer to fighters. He arrived at *Jasta* 27 on 12 September, and only four days later claimed a Sopwith shot down near Ypres. That claim remained unconfirmed, but Klimke was luckier on the 26th. On that date he successfully claimed two Sopwiths to bring his score to four.

On 20 October Göring was awarded the 'Hohenzollern'. During the afternoon of the 21st, Goring led a six-aeroplane *Kette* (a flight of three to six aircraft) down on a similar number of No 84 Sqn SE 5 as that were attacking a two-seater LVG. Göring achieved his

The Albatros fighters of *Jasta* 27 are seen at Iseghem in the summer of 1917. Göring's D V 1027/17 is at left, marked with a black fuselage and white nose and tail. Next is an Albatros D III numbered '1', then a D V numbered '2'. It is presumed that the other aircraft have black fuselages with black numbers on white bands

15th victory, and the 28th for *Jasta* 27, by downing one of the RFC scouts. Dilthey downed two Sopwiths in October to bring his tally to four, while Klimke 'made ace' on the 24th.

On 1 November *Jasta* 27 moved from Iseghem to Bavichove. As the weather worsened the *Staffel* recorded fewer combats, with four enemy aeroplanes downed in November and December. At some point in late November Göring went on leave, and Dilthey was acting commander in his absence. Klimke contributed one of the unit's four January victories to bring his total to six.

Slated for inclusion in JG III, *Jasta* 27 was also expected to receive Fokker triplanes. However, sufficient numbers were not available and the *Staffel* would perform its first duties in the *Geschwader* equipped with Albatros types. On 13 February 1918, having achieved about 40 victories, *Jasta* 27 relocated to Marckebeeke airfield to join the other JG III components in the area near Courtrai.

JASTA 36

Jagdstaffel 36 was officially established on 11 January 1917 and was activated at *FEA* 13 in Breslau on 21 February. On that date its first CO, Ltn d R Albert Dossenbach, arrived from *Jasta* 'Boelcke'. At this time he had downed nine Allied aircraft as a two-seater pilot and included among his many decorations the *Pour le Mérite*. His new *Jasta* was ordered to *AFP* 3 at Rethel, where a complement of Albatros D IIIs was acquired. The unit's first operational aerodrome was at Le Châtelet in the 3rd Army sector, but this unprepared location required two weeks of construction to create the required facilities to turn it into an airfield – the unit's OzbV (officer for special duties, or adjutant), Ltn d R Aristides Müller, worked hard to get this accomplished. On 11 March Ltn d R Heinrich Bongartz arrived, and his talents and iron will would prove essential to the unit's success.

Like his close friend Paul Bäumer, Bongartz was a Westphalian, born in Gelsenkirchen on 31 January 1892. He started his war service in *Reserve-Infanterie-Regt Nr* 13, and he was commissioned in March 1916 during the bloody struggle at Verdun. After applying for a transfer to the Air Service Bongartz was posted to *FFA* 5 at Hannover in July 1916 and qualified as a pilot in August. His daring attitude made quite an impression on his commander Hptm Krüger, who is said to have written in his evaluation, 'A dead-certain candidate for the *Pour le Mérite*, if his audacity does not get him shot down first'. This was a prophetic statement indeed. October 1916 found Bongartz flying with *Kasta* 27 of *Kagohl* 5, which was renamed *Schutzstaffel* 8 at year end. He then switched to fighters and joined *Jasta* 36.

Dossenbach's new *Staffel* flew its initial sorties against the French on 16 March 1917. The first confirmed victory went to the CO when he destroyed a Caudron G IV

Ltn d R Heinrich Bongartz was the preeminent *Jagdflieger* of *Jasta* 36. Here, he poses with his Albatros D III 607/17 circa April 1917 – it was marked only with a personal fuselage band in the proportions of the Iron Cross ribbon. Bongartz scored the first of his victories in 'Bloody April'. All of his successes (variously recorded as 33 or 34) were tallied with *Jasta* 36, constituting about 25 per cent of the unit's total (*L Bronnenkant*)

from *Escadrille* C39 on 5 April. The next day two other *Jasta* 36 pilots chalked up their first *Luftsieg*, while Dossenbach claimed a Nieuport that went unconfirmed. Bongartz was apparently the victor over a SPAD VII flown by Lt Mistarlet of *Escadrille* 31.

During April 1917 the *Staffel* was credited with 13 French aeroplanes, as well as two balloons flamed by Bongartz. However, on 2 May a French bomb raid on the *Jasta* 36 field left Dossenbach badly wounded and he left for a field hospital. The *Jasta* relocated to St Loup on 4 May, and six days later Ltn Walter von Bülow-Bothkamp arrived from *Jasta* 18 to take command. The *Jasta* flourished under his leadership, with Bongartz adding four more victories to his string in May.

A future *Jasta* 36 ace who started scoring in May was Ltn d R Theodor Quandt. Born in East Prussia on 22 June 1897, Quandt was a veteran of *Feld-Artillerie Regt Nr* 20. Commissioned on 29 February 1916, he switched to aviation on 1 July. On the first day of 1917 he joined *FA (A)* 270 and flew with that unit until posted to *Jasta* 36 on 27 March. He destroyed two balloons in May, and claimed a SPAD that went unconfirmed.

On 18 June 1917 the *Jasta* received orders to go to Sailly in the 4th Army Sector, and six days later it was ordered to Marckebeeke, near Courtrai – opposite the RFC on the fiercely-contested Flanders Front. Following a move to Kuerne airfield, Bongartz accounted for three aeroplanes in early July. On the unlucky 'Friday the 13th' of that month, however, Bongartz was badly wounded in the arm during an attack on a British bomber and left for one of his many stays in hospital. In August *Jasta* 36 accounted for four more opponents, one of which was a No 21 Sqn RE 8 destroyed by Quandt on 11 July for his third 'kill'.

After a spell of bad weather the *Staffel* resumed its success with three victories on 3 September, with von Bülow getting his 18th and Quandt his fourth. On 7 September the CO's brother, Ltn d R Harry von Bülow, was welcomed into the *Jasta* ranks. Harry had been born on the family's estate in Bothkamp, Holstein, on 19 November 1897. He went to war as a 17-year-old volunteer with *Königlich Sächsischen Husaren-Regt Nr* 18 and was commissioned on 23 May 1916. Many years later von Bülow wrote a brief autobiographical sketch for an American historian;

'I learned to fly in August 1916 and was first assigned to *FEA* 10 at Böblingen, before transferring to *FA* 53 in December 1916. This squadron was later re-numbered *FA* 272(A) under the command of Hptm Kleine. In August 1917 I went through the fighter training school in Valenciennes and in September 1917 I was posted to *Jagdstaffel* 36, then commanded by my brother Walter. Walter soon took over command of *Jagdstaffel* "Boelcke", and I served with that squadron from 2 January until 11 March 1918. My brother was killed in combat near Ypres on 6 January 1918 and I was then re-transferred to *Jasta* 36 on 11 March. I was squadron commander of this unit until 15 August 1918, being withdrawn from the front when the last of my brothers fell in action. The English pursuit pilots titled our group "the Blue Noses", from which you can conclude that the noses of *Jasta* 36 aircraft were painted blue.'

Pilots of *Jasta* 36 pose with their commander at Kuerne airfield. Their identities are believed to be, from left to right, Ltn Günther Lüdecke, Vzfw Egon Patzer, Ltn d R Bongartz, Ltn Hans Denkewitz, Ltn Max Führmann, Ltn Walter von Bülow-Bothkamp (with the 'Blue Max' at his throat), Ltn Hans Hoyer, Ltn d R Harry von Bülow-Bothkamp, Ltn d R Aristides Müller (OzbV) arm-in-arm with Ltn d R Hans Gottfried von Häbler, Ltn d R Theodor Quandt and Ltn d R Hans Böhning. Some historians believe that the names of Hoyer and Fuhrmann have been switched, which is possible (*L Bronnenkant*)

On 13 September Bongartz returned. He was on his way to a reputation as one of the 'iron men' of the Air Service for his ability to recover from multiple wounds.

On the morning of 17 September there was a scrap between Bristol F 2B Fighters of No 20 Sqn and *Jasta* 36 over Poelcapelle. Quandt apparently shot down the F 2B flown by Capt A G V Taylor (seven victories) and his observer, Sgt Benger (both crewmen died of their wounds), while Bongartz shot up another of the two-seaters. The latter enjoyed yet more success on 26 September, when he, Quandt, Ltn d R Hans Böhning and Walter von Bülow each chalked up a victory.

Four days later Ltn d R Hans Gottfried von Häbler arrived from *Jastaschule* I. Born in Gross Schonau in Saxony on 17 May 1893, the young nobleman had enlisted in the elite *Königlich Sächsisches Garde-Reiter-Regt (1. Schweres Regt)* on 1 October 1913 in Dresden. After two years of frontline service he transferred to aviation and was posted to *FEA* 9 sometime in the autumn of 1916. September 1917 found von Häbler serving as a pilot in *FA* 273(A), before being sent to *Jastaschule* I. He wasted no time starting his career as a *Jagdflieger,* destroying a Bristol F 2B Fighter from No 22 Sqn on the morning of 7 October. The F 2B was crewed by pilot 2Lt J C Bush MC (an ace with seven victories) and Lt W W Chapman, both of whom were killed.

The 31 October entry in the *Staffel* war diary recorded Bongartz' 20th victory;

'In the afternoon all ten machines take off again, and again there are victors! Ltn Bongartz shoots down a Sopwith on the Roulers-Menin Road at 1600 hrs, which brings him his 20th recognised victory and the 64th for the *Staffel.* A little later Ltn d R [Hans] Hoyer defeats a SPAD near Kezelberg – his seventh victory, and the 65th victory for the *Staffel.*'

In November the *Jasta* frequently tangled with No 65 Sqn, and its brilliantly decorated Albatros fighters left a vivid impression on the unit's opponents. In 1971, Camel pilot Guy M Knocker recalled a typical November dogfight, stating, 'and then all around comes the well-known whip-like cracking and the streams of tracer as Albatri come clattering down. I can see their black and white chequered wings and hooped fuselages and recognise them as what we call von Bülow's Circus.'

Bongartz later wrote a vivid (although undated) description of the fierce encounters over Flanders typical of this era, and of the *Geschwader* period that followed;

'In the afternoon at around five o'clock the German and English fighter pilots in Flanders met regularly for "five o'clock tea" between Houthulst Wood and Zillebeke Lake. Hard toast was served. These meetings became so popular that in the end one was able to speak of mass visits – 50 to 60 aircraft on each side in close formation. Like elsewhere on the front, one could only achieve victories over the strong enemy forces if one succeeded in bringing one's own aircraft into a favourable attack position above the enemy aircraft. Both

These highly decorated Albatros D V and D III fighters of *Jasta* 36 reveal why the unit was known to some of its RFC opponents as 'von Bülow's Circus'. The first four aircraft are Albatros D V types, but the next is a chequerboard-painted D III. In late September 1917, *Jasta* 36 became part of *Jagdgruppe* 4, together with *Jastas* 'Boelcke', 26 and 27, and battled the RFC relentlessly in the skies over Flanders

sides knew this. Therefore, each formation attempted to climb above the other. One could not properly come to grips with one's slippery opponent.

'We were all fed up with waltzing along the front with the Englishmen. Then Göring [*Jasta* 26] came up with a bold plan – we were to place a decoy before the Englishman's nose and then nab him. One group cruised from Houthulst Wood to Zillebeke Lake and the other did the opposite, so that both sides would meet in the middle between the wood and the lake at different altitudes.

'At that time I had the newest and fastest machine, and I therefore took on the job of providing the lure. After takeoff I swung in a large arc towards Nieuport and climbed to a considerable height. Then I flew towards Zillebeke Lake in such a way that I came upon the Englishmen beneath me from out of the glaring sun, which was at my back. At first they may have taken me for a compatriot, but then recognised me as I drew closer. An attempt was made to circle up towards me.

'During this circus flying I thrusted twice towards the English leader without firing, but each time he evaded me. But then when I saw one of our groups gliding dangerously close beneath the cockade-bearing machines, I suddenly commenced a third attack, and it succeeded. As I put my aeroplane on its nose it tore down like a saw, and I "spat" at the Englishman from both guns. I gave him the works, and he fell apart in flames. At the same time, as the English propellers and machine guns took aim at me as if on command, I succeeded in dashing with my swift machine through the gap which my downed opponent left behind.

'The Englishmen came after me. They fired like mad, without scoring a hit. They posed a greater danger to themselves than to me. At the same time they were caught in our trap and, because we had a "Joffre wind" coming from France, they were almost automatically blown into it. Our *Staffeln* sunk their teeth into their necks. After the first aircraft went down, the enemy fell into disarray. All of them scattered like chaff in the wind in order to reach their own lines. Smouldering and flaming clumps separated themselves from the tumult. Burning wings fluttered down. When I inspected my machine after landing, I did not find a single hit, despite the witches' cauldron into which I had gotten myself.'

Bongartz received the 'Hohenzollern' on 24 November, and only three days later the *Jasta 36* war diary recorded;

'Ltn Bongartz shoots down a Sopwith, but this one rams a second one and takes him into the depths – [his] 24th and 25th victories and 75th and 76th *Staffel* victories. In the afternoon *Kette* "von Bülow" flies. Walter von Bülow shoots down a Sopwith at Passchendaele and wins his 27th victory [and] the 77th *Staffel* victory.'

Bongartz' unlucky victims were two Camels from No 65 Sqn that collided as one was trying to escape from his fire, and von Bülow's opponent was also from the same unit.

On 13 December Walter von Bülow left to take over *Jasta* 'Boelcke' (with whom he was killed in action on 6 January 1918), and leadership of *Jasta 36* passed to Bongartz. It seems that it was Bongartz who instituted the *Staffel* marking of blue noses for aircraft of his unit.

18 December 1917 was another great day for *Jasta 36* and a black one for No 65 Sqn. In a letter written the next day, Hans von Häbler reported;

One of *Jasta* 36's most successful Albatros exponents was Ltn d R Hans Gottfried von Häbler. Prior to joining the unit, he had been awarded the Saxon Knight's Cross of the Military St Henry Order for an extremely long-range reconnaissance flight made on 10 September 1917 as a pilot in *Flieger-Abteilung (A) 273*. Only a week after his arrival in *Jasta* 36 von Häbler chalked up his first victory when he downed a Bristol F 2B Fighter on 7 October 1917. On 18 December his score reached six when he downed Sopwith Camel B2388 of No 64 Sqn – he befriended the captured pilot, 2Lt R H 'Bob' Cowan. Long after von Häbler's death, Cowan would establish a close friendship with his father in 1931 (*S K Taylor*)

'Yesterday I was rather successful in bringing down two English aeroplanes. In the forenoon, I had first followed Bongartz who, however, had to return – his motor having become defective – so I continued on my way alone. I went a little way off when I made out an RE coming to the front. First I kept up my direction as if I had not seen it. A thousand metres above the RE there were four Sopwiths. When the RE reached the front, I turned around and was very quickly behind it. I fired and down it went vertically [the RE 8 was from No 21 Sqn, its crew being killed]. I got another chance and it plunged down burning, but unfortunately it can't be helped. Meanwhile, one of the four Sopwiths had come down, but it did not come near.

'In the afternoon we were flying, six of us in a *Kette,* when we perceived 15 Sopwiths on the German side. I scarcely trusted my eyes. Wherever you looked there were cockades. Bongartz and I were the first to attack. We were at once in the middle of it, and it was a throng like at a fair. After I had fired off at different aircraft I got one fast and got him out of the throng. I had many gun stoppages, else I would have done it in a shorter time. So we flew for about ten minutes in curves until he landed on our side and was wrecked. I hope he is alive. Bongartz got his down as well.'

Von Häbler's opponent – Canadian 2Lt Robert Cowan of No 65 Sqn – was indeed alive, as was Bongartz' victim, 2Lt Cameron. The next day von Häbler wrote;

'When I found out that my Englishman of the day before yesterday was not badly wounded, and captive at the *Fluna* (intelligence HQ), I went there with [OzbV] Müller. His name is R H Cowan, 18 years old, only a fortnight at the front and such a nice, neat boy! He told us another [English squadron] had shot down four aircraft, so they wanted to do the same. Then I had come and shot his machine to pieces. With that, he was lucky my machine gun was out of order or else he would not have been alive. Anyway, I was so happy that he was! He was really a nice, kind, gentlemanly, boy. When he heard that I had shot down six aeroplanes he said, "Very good!" So that is all.'

During their friendly meeting Cowan presented von Häbler with his flying helmet as a souvenir. The Canadian spent the rest of the war in a PoW camp, but von Häbler was mortally wounded by flak on 22 March 1918 and died in captivity the following day. In 1931, Cowan, with fond memories of his victor, succeeded in making contact with the late German ace's father. The elder von Häbler was delighted to be in touch with Cowan, and a lengthy and touching exchange of letters and photographs followed. According to Canadian historian Stewart Taylor, Cowan became almost a 'surrogate son' for von Häbler's father, but sadly their correspondence was ended with the advent of the Nazi regime.

Bongartz, with his score at 27, received his *Pour le Mérite* on 23 December 1917 from the Kaiser himself, after which he went on leave. The next day Quandt left the *Staffel* to take over the new *Jasta* 53, but he would later return. 1917 ended with a *Staffel* tally of 87 confirmed victories. By the end of January 1918 the unit had acquired a number of Fokker Dr I triplanes. Bongartz was also back, having returned from leave on 21 January 1918. With stalwarts such as Bongartz and von Häbler in their ranks and equipped with the Fokker Dr I, the *Jasta* 36 pilots could look with pride at their record and anticipate more triumphs ahead.

CHAPTER TWO

KAISERSCHLACHT

Jagdgeschwader Nr III was written into existence on 2 February 1918 in the German 4th Army sector pursuant to the orders of *Kriegsministerium Nr* 4524.18. A7L. It is believed that Oblt Bruno Loerzer was named commander at this time. However, the complex logistical and administrative tasks associated with bringing such a large new formation to operational status would take nearly two weeks.

On 12 February, Loerzer took a break from his work to receive his hard-won *Pour le Mérite,* presented in a chilly ceremony by Kaiser Wilhelm II. Loerzer continued flying and fighting as leader of *Jasta* 26 as he also dealt with the practical problems of bringing four *Staffeln* together into a functional combat unit. All of the *Jastas* were to be based in the vicinity of Courtrai, and *Jasta* 36 was already in place at Kuerne airfield. On 11 February *Jasta* 26 made the move from Bavichove to Marckebeeke, where Göring's *Jasta* 27 joined them on the 13th. Three days later *Jasta* 'Boelcke' also left Bavichove and moved its triplanes and personnel to Marcke. Ltn d R Fritz Loerzer was transferred from *Jasta* 63 to take over the helm of *Jasta* 26 from his elder brother on 20 February. That same day Oblt Carl Bolle was placed in command of *Jasta* 'Boelcke'.

About seven months later, a weekly report issued by the *Kofl* of the 17th Army (for 11-18 September 1918) stated that the first victory claimed by JG III came on 18 February 1918. Therefore, we will provisionally date the operational history of JG III as starting on that date (appropriately,

On a chilly day in February 1918, Oblt Bruno Loerzer (at right, saluting) received his *Pour le Mérite* from the hands of Kaiser Wilhelm II himself (centre). The date of Loerzer's award is recorded as 12 February, and he may have still been in Berlin, as this was the last day of the fighter trials that he was attending there. He had scored his 20th victory on 19 January, which was the usual benchmark for recommendation for the Order (*L Bronnenkant*)

Bruno Loerzer scored his 23rd victory that day when he downed a Camel). Other documents record Loerzer as taking command of JG III on 21 February 1918. Oblt Theodor Hermann Dahlmann, a veteran officer with one victory scored with *Jasta* 29, would later serve as the OzbV for *Geschwader*.

All four of the *Staffeln* limited their activities somewhat in the following weeks in order to conserve aircraft, fuel and other resources in readiness for the coming offensive. Carl Bolle, who had just been transferred in to lead *Jasta* 'B', and at this time had 'only' five victories, described his appointment (writing in the third person) and the days that followed;

'To commission a pilot who had been flying in Flanders for about a year, but until now could only show five aerial victories, with the leadership of this *Staffel* was a risk. At least, experience and trust could be taken for granted. In this respect, the new leader found favourable conditions as he encountered a group of experienced pilots and, simultaneously, the organisation of *Jagdgeschwader Nr* III – to which *Jagdstaffel* "Boelcke" now belonged – and he had a period of quiet for a certain span of time. The transfer to the staging areas for the "Great Battle" in France that followed shortly afterwards, and the corresponding scaling back of aerial activities, provided leader and *Staffel* with the leisure to get used to one another.'

Born in Berlin on 20 June 1893, Bolle was an avid athlete as a student, participating in ice hockey and rowing. He attended Oxford University, before returning to Germany in 1913 and enlisting in an elite cuirassier regiment – he subsequently went to war with that unit. Bolle began his flight training at Johannisthal in early 1916, and by July was flying with *Kagohl* IV. In October he was wounded when his machine was attacked by five French fighters, but he succeeded in bringing his crippled aeroplane down in German lines and helping his wounded observer to safety. Following his recovery Bolle was posted to *Jasta* 28, where he gained his initial victories.

In spite of the 'scaling back of aerial activities', there were still opportunities to add to one's victory list. On 21 February, Hermann Göring led Rudolf Klimke and two others from *Jasta* 27 into action against a patrol of nine scouts from No 60 Sqn, and both of the German aces achieved credit for an SE 5a. Göring wrote a typically hyperbolic tale of this action for a 1933 issue of the British periodical *Popular Flying*, in which he exaggerated the qualities of his opponent to embellish his own achievement;

'What a battle it was! First up, then down – at the moment we were at a height of 4500 metres, the next we had fallen to 2000, only to climb back to 3000. Without resting for a moment our machine guns blazed at each other. Then at a height of about 1000 metres, by making an unexpected right-hand turn, I managed to come round on the tail of my opponent and give him full fire at close range. This manoeuvre won me the fight. He fell, his engine going full out as he plunged headlong to earth.

'From the papers we found on his body we learnt that my brave adversary was no less a person than the famous Capt Craig, known all along the line for his audacity and daring.'

In reality, the pilot was Canadian 2Lt G B Craig – no doubt a courageous airman, but one of no great reputation – who died of his wounds the next day. His companion, 2Lt William M Kent, was killed in the combat, being credited to Klimke. However, historian Stewart Taylor researched No 60 Sqn records of this action and believes that the two SE 5a pilots actually collided with each other during the combat.

In late February poor weather hampered operations, but the sky cleared enough on the 24th for Ltn d R Wilhelm Papenmeyer of *Jasta* 'B' to earn credit for an RE 8 downed near St Julien. Two days later his *Staffel* comrade Richard Plange used his Fokker Dr I to claim a 'SPAD', which was probably one of No 19 Sqn's new (and unfamiliar) Sopwith

On 24 February 1918, Wilhelm Papenmeyer of *Jasta* 'Boelcke' downed an RE 8 for his third victory, and two days later Richard Plange also racked up his third. The pilots of *Jasta* 'B' display their prized walking sticks (gifts from Anthony Fokker) and an obvious *esprit de corps* in this photo, taken circa late February. From left to right in the front row are Hermann Vallendor, Paul Schröder, *Staffelführer* Carl Bolle, Plange and Papenmeyer. In the back row are Otto Löffler, Fritz Kempf, Harry von Bülow-Bothkamp, Karl Gallwitz and Paul Bäumer. As Bolle himself wrote, the fighting strength of *Jasta* 'B' rarely exceeded ten pilots. Nevertheless, the cumulative score of the group pictured here was 131 victories. Only Papenmeyer and Plange would not survive the war

Dolphins, for his third victory. On 8 March, No 19 Sqn encountered JG III aircraft again, but this time Albatros pilot Offz Stv Willi Kampe of *Jasta* 27 was killed – nonetheless, he was posthumously credited with his eighth victory during this fight. On the 9th, flying his Dr I 204/17, Paul Bäumer successfully claimed a Sopwith for his 19th victory. However, that same day Ltn d R Max Naujok of *Jasta* 36 was forced to crash land in his Dr I after a long dogfight. His triplane hit a tree and he was later discovered dead with a fractured skull.

For the planned Spring Offensive, JG III was assigned to the 17th Army, commanded by *General der Infanterie* Otto von Below. From 12 to 15 March, all four *Staffeln* were occupied in moving about 50 kilometres from their aerodromes near Courtrai, Belgium, in the 4th Army sector to a large area of flat farmland west of the French village of Erchin (southeast of Douai). In common with other aviation units being moved in for the coming offensive, JG III did its best to prevent its existence from being discovered by Allied reconnaissance aircraft. Pitching hangar tents was forbidden, and the aeroplanes were stored in farm buildings in the area. Operations were limited to a few flights in order to allow pilots to familiarise themselves with the area. Hangar tents would not be erected until the evening of 21 March – the first day of the assault. In preparation for participation in the offensive, the 17th Army had nine other *Jagdstaffeln* at its disposal, along with the four from JG III.

DER TAG

At 0445 hrs on the morning of 21 March 1918, nearly 10,000 German guns and mortars opened fire to begin Operation *Michael,* the first of the offensives devised by *Generalquartiermeister* Erich Ludendorff that would become known as *Kaiserschlacht* (the Imperial Battle or Emperor's Battle). This was an attack on a massive scale, stretching from the River Scarpe in the north to the River Serre in the south. At 0945 hrs the German infantry began their assault through thick fog. That same fog and low clouds prevented the aerial forces in the 17th Army sector from participating in the attack until nearly midday. *Jasta* 27 patrols led by

As the Spring Offensive opened on 21 March 1918, *Jasta* 26 was still largely equipped with Albatros fighters, while *Jastas* 'Boelcke' and 36 had Fokker Dr Is. These *Jasta* 26 D Va types are representative of the unit's equipment at this time. The aircraft marked 'X' at left may have had the serial number 5663/17, but that is not confirmed. The X marking was repeated on the underside of the starboard bottom wing

On 23 March 1918, Bruno Loerzer achieved his 23rd victory. He is seen at right during a visit from Crown Prince Wilhelm (centre). In the background is Loerzer's D Va 5602/17, in typical *Jasta* 26 colours. The other men are members of *Flieger-Abteilung (A)* 274 – the unit formerly known as *FFA 25* – in which both Loerzer and Göring got their start. This group had a long association with the *Kronprinz*. From left, they are identified as *Freiherr* von Cobeltitz, Ltn d R Julius *Graf* von Schaesburg-Thannheim, Uffz Wilhelm Hübener, the Crown Prince, Hptm Schubert and Loerzer (*L Bronnenkant*)

Göring in the afternoon and early evening encountered no resistance. The heavy concentration of German fighters ensured aerial supremacy, allowing the army co-operation two-seaters to carry out their missions with little interference from RFC aircraft.

From midday on the 22nd an increase in RFC activity was perceived, especially on the 17th Army front where the British were expected to do their best to hold on to Arras. In the afternoon JG III pilots engaged RFC squadrons over the Cambrai region in a fiercely-contested battle and succeeded in breaking up the British formations. Sopwiths (possibly from No 70 Sqn) were credited to *Staffelführer* Fritz Loerzer and Otto Esswein of *Jasta* 26. However, *Jasta* 36 suffered a crippling loss when the aristocratic ace Hans Gottfried von Häbler failed to return. The *Jasta* 36 diary states his Fokker Dr I was brought down by ground fire behind British lines during an aerial engagement. Five days later, the diarist wrote, 'Due to the advance of the ground troops during the offensive Ltn von Häbler's Fokker Dr I 509/17 was found intact, and it is believed the best may be hoped for and that he is a prisoner and alive'. Sadly, it was not so – von Häbler had died of his wounds in a British hospital on the 23rd.

That same day the RFC concentrated on attacking army co-operation aeroplanes east of Bapaume. Once again pilots from JG III and other units fought ceaselessly to drive back the British squadrons. At 0835 hrs,

Jasta 27's Klimke claimed an SE 5a at Hendecourt for his eighth victory. In the afternoon, Paul Bäumer had taken off in his reserve Albatros, and when he became separated from the other members of his *Staffel* he joined up with a *Jasta* 36 patrol. Between 1300 hrs and 1330 hrs, the group attacked a formation of five Camels from No 46 Sqn – Bongartz downed one of them at Lagnicourt (his 31st victory) and Bäumer of *Jasta* 'B' got another (his 20th). *Geschwaderführer* Bruno Loerzer, who was never one to lead from behind his desk, also claimed a Camel at 1440 hrs.

About one hour later Bäumer was aloft again, attacking an RE 8 at 800 metres and bringing it down north of Tilloy. He shot another of the same type down in flames at 1615 hrs, north of Beugnatre. Fritz Loerzer achieved his ninth victory with a Sopwith, while his fellow *Jasta* 26 pilot Vzfw Fritz Beckhardt claimed an SE 5a that went unconfirmed. JG III's tally for the day was an impressive nine credited victories (with no casualties). However, the other *Jastas* ordered to deal with low-flying enemies were

In another photo taken during the Crown Prince's visit, Loerzer leans over the cockpit to explain the controls to his royal visitor, who stands beside D Va 5602/17 and glances at the camera. A lengthwise black stripe was painted on the pale blue underside of the bottom wings, probably as a leader's marking

not so successful and British aeroplanes were observed attacking German troops for the first time.

A strong reinforcement of British squadrons in the sector was noticed on 24-25 March, which presented more obstacles to the 17th Army *Jagdstaffeln*. Formations of up 60 enemy aeroplanes were seen on the morning of the 26th – the day historian Trevor Henshaw has called 'the most crucial day of air fighting' of the offensive. The largest British air concentration of the war thus far was thrown against the Germans, and JG III pilots again went into the fray in a day of intense and chaotic combat.

At 1700 hrs, Ltn d R Fritz Paul 'Claus' Riemer of *Jasta* 26 claimed an SE 5a near Bihucourt for his first victory, and Otto Fruhner claimed another 20 minutes later (these may reflect losses by No 1 Sqn). Pilots from *Jastas* 'Boelcke' and 26 seem to have engaged Sopwith Dolphins from No 19 Sqn from 1700 hrs to 1730 hrs, although the fighters were misidentified as Martinsydes. *Jasta* 26 pilots Esswein and Ltn Helmut Lange each achieved a *Luftsieg*, while Vzfw Erich Buder brought down a No 52 Sqn RE 8 for the first of at least twelve victories for him. In addition, Richard Plange from *Jasta* 'Boelcke' also shot up a 'Martinsyde' at Grevillers Forest for his fourth confirmed opponent. This was recorded as *Jasta* 'Boelcke's' 200th victory at the time in the unit's war diary, and some merry celebrations must have ensued.

The triplane pilots of *Jasta* 'Boelcke' were highly successful during the early days of *Kaiserschlacht*. On 27 March, Gallwitz and Vallendor each attained confirmed victories while Plange recorded two. This is Paul Schröder's Dr I 157/17, now displaying the black(?) and white striped interplane struts along with a narrowly-outlined rudder and other typical *Jasta* 'B' décor

27 March brought no respite. Vzfw Alfred Hübner of *Jasta* 36 recorded his first victory with a 'Bristol' near Avéluy Wood, which may have been a DH 4 lost by No 25 Sqn that morning. At 0755 hrs *Jasta* 36's hard-driving leader Bongartz claimed another 'Bristol' near Albert, followed by a Sopwith five minutes later to bring his total to 33. At about 1100 hrs Ltn Karl Gallwitz of *Jasta* 'B' shot down a Bristol from No 20 Sqn for his eighth victory – it was flown by Capts Kirkham and Hedley, who were both taken prisoner. Richard Plange shot down an RE 8 south of Albert for his fifth, and was also part of a flight of seven triplanes

from *Jasta* 'Boelcke' that attacked ten SE 5as from No 56 Sqn engaged in strafing ground targets near Morlancourt. In this fight Ltn d R Hermann Vallendor and Plange were both credited with SEs, Vallendor shooting down Lt Stewart Maxwell in flames for his second kill.

Hermann Vallendor was born in Offenberg, in Baden, on 13 April 1894. After studying engineering he joined *Infanterie Regt Nr* 114 on 16 October 1914. Vallendor rose through the ranks until he was commissioned on Christmas Eve 1915. He applied for a transfer to aviation, and was sent to train at *FEA* 5 on 16 October 1916. May 1917 found Vallendor flying in *FA* 23, and on 24 June he was posted to the *Jastaschule* for transition to fighters. Receiving his pilot's badge on 4 July, Vallendor arrived at the 'Boelcke' *Staffel* the very next day

28 March brought disaster for the closely-knit circle of *Jasta* 'Boelcke' pilots. Flying Fokker Dr I 409/17, Ltn d R Wilhelm Papenmeyer had attacked an RE 8 at about 1020 hrs. It seems he shot it down, but its observer managed to shoot up the triplane before dying. Papenmeyer brought his Dr I down in no-man's land near Acheville and, badly wounded, exited the aircraft. Somehow he crawled to a nearby shell hole or trench, where he bled to death. His body was found a few days later by advancing German infantry.

The German advance ground to a halt on 28 March, and successes for JG III proved elusive in the succeeding days. A consignment of Fokker Dr Is reached the unit at around this time, but there were not enough to fully equip both *Jastas* 26 and 27. *Jasta* 26 acquired a full complement of triplanes but *Jasta* 27 could only provide Dr Is for about half of its pilots, with the rest forced to continue flying Albatros fighters. Ace Ltn d R Helmut Dilthey was amongst the small number of pilots in the unit to be issued with a Fokker fighter;

'It became somewhat better when we received triplanes. At that time they were no longer as good as the British single- and two-seaters. Above all, they were too slow and the engines were too temperamental. Other than that, they were quite lovely. Our triplanes had yellow cowlings, yellow interplane struts, yellow tails and were in other respects in natural [factory] colours. Our Albatros biplanes, which we still had in April 1918, were black with yellow tails and yellow engine cowlings. Only Oblt Göring's leader's aircraft had a white tail and a white cowling.'

Dilthey, who would leave *Jasta* 27 on 14 April for *Jasta* 40, was killed in action on 9 July.

On 30 March, Bongartz was, according to historian Alex Imrie, very lightly wounded by flak whilst flying Dr I 441/17. Photographs reveal that the entire leading edge of his triplane's upper wing was shredded – possibly by the same shell burst – but he still landed safely, and he stayed with his unit. On that same day Riemer of *Jasta* 26 shot up an SE 5a from No 1 Sqn at 0720 hrs for his first claim – 2Lt Sweeting was

In late March, a consignment of Dr Is arrived for JG III, permitting *Jasta* 26 to be fully equipped with triplanes, while the remainder went to *Jasta* 27. This *Jasta* 26 aircraft in full unit markings made a forced landing south of Achiet-le-Petit, 12 kilometres from Bapaume, in late March. It displays a personal emblem of a 'V' in black(?) on the sides and top of the fuselage and in white on the centre section of the top wing. The white cross fields on the upper wing have been painted over in a solid camouflage colour to produce the required narrow white cross borders, and this has been carried out on the bottom wing insignia as well *(courtesy R Absmeier)*

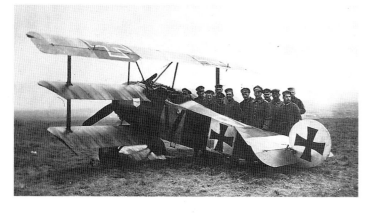

wounded but returned safely to his lines. Riemer had trained at *FEA* 13 from August 1917 to 27 February 1918, when he was posted to *AFP* 6 and then on to *Jastaschule* I. On 12 March 1918 he arrived at *Staffel* 26 and would stay with the unit until war's end, attaining seven victories.

On 1 April 1918 the RFC was amalgamated with the RNAS to form the new Royal Air Force (RAF), but at the time such details mattered little to either the British

On 30 March 1918, *Jasta* 36 commander Bongartz was wounded by a burst of flak while flying Dr I 441/17, but he landed the triplane safely. The entire leading edge of the upper wing broke up, and this view shows the loose and torn fabric on that component. A section of the wing's leading edge plywood came off and was wedged in the starboard centre-section struts. The Iron Cross insignia marked on the tailplane was a near universal facet of *Jasta* 36 Dr Is, along with their blue engine cowlings (*M Thiemeyer*)

or German airmen involved in the intense combat in the skies over Picardy.

This day saw the first *Luftsieg* for Vzfw Albert Lux of *Jasta* 27. Lux had a long history in German aviation. After attending flying schools in Grossenhain and Travemünde, he flew as a frontline pilot with *Schutzstaffel* 13 from 10 February 1917 to 4 April. At that point he was transferred to *FA* 293(A) and flew artillery-spotting missions until 9 October 1917, when he was posted to *AFP* 4. After a brief five-day course at *Jastaschule* I, Lux returned to *AFP* 4 before arriving at *Jasta* 27 on 17 November 1917. Although he had taken four months to chalk up his first victory, his scoring would accelerate considerably in the summer after acquiring the Fokker D VII.

Göring increased his tally at midday on 7 April, when he led nine other *Jasta* 27 pilots in attacking an RE 8 and some escorting fighters near Merville, about 25 kilometres inside the British lines. The No 42 Sqn aeroplane was 'forced down' by Göring for his 18th credit and his unit's 49th, although the two-seater actually managed to return to its airfield. The crew reported that they had been attacked by 'six triplanes and four Albatros scouts'.

9 April 1918 saw the beginning of the second Ludendorff offensive by the 6th Army, known variously as Operation *Georgette* or the Battle of the Lys. The next day, Paul Bäumer was finally commissioned as a leutnant in the reserves after obtaining 22 confirmed 'kills'. On 11 April Vzfw Fritz Beckhardt, the Jewish pilot of *Jasta* 26, downed an RE 8 at Bethune for his first confirmed victory. The following day JG III was

The pilot of this blue-nosed *Jasta* 36 Dr I is unknown. His personal emblem was the zigzag line on a white band. In common with many *Jasta* 'Boelcke' triplanes, this aircraft's white rudder has been outlined in black

on the move again, this time back to the 4th Army sector in preparation for the approaching Kemmel Offensive (the Battle for Kemmel Ridge) in Flanders. In this phase of *Georgette,* the 4th Army's goal was to take Mount Kemmel, a 159-metre-high ridge that would allow the Germans to shell the channel ports. Between the 12th and the 17th the *Geschwader* moved north to the aerodrome at Halluin-Ost.

On 21 April, Ltn d R Gallwitz shot down a 'Sopwith' west of Bailleul – his ninth victory in the *Jasta* 'Boelcke' war diary. That same day, of course, former *Jasta* 'B' pilot and current JG I commander Manfred von Richthofen was killed at Vaux sur

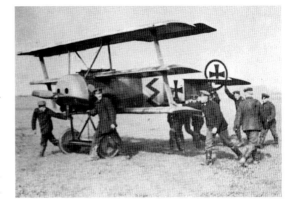

Somme. The next day, Göring was at the controls of Dr I 496/17 as he led nine pilots of *Jasta* 27 back to their field. When landing, he was seemingly caught in a crosswind and flew the triplane into a hangar, writing it off.

On preparation for the 4th Army attack on Mount Kemmel, Hptm Bruno Loerzer was given control of ten *Jagdstaffeln* organised into two *Jagdgruppen*, in addition to the four *Jastas* of his own JG III. Loerzer worked tirelessly with *Kofl* 4, Hptm Wilberg, to coordinate the efforts of these *Staffeln* and ensure that their pilots were well trained and prepared for their assignments. Of the Air Service's achievements in the Kemmel offensive, *Kogenluft* Ernst von Hoeppner would write, 'The general use of aviation in this battle was exemplary due to the carefully conceived arrangements made by the *Kofl* of the 4th Army. The 14 *Staffeln* under the command of *Jagdgeschwader Nr* III operated in a zone that was only 15 kilometres wide, and flew far into the enemy's rear areas.'

The attack on Mount Kemmel was launched with three divisions on 25 April 1918. That morning the *Jasta* 36 diary reported that there was a gigantic ground battle raging near Mount Kemmel, and flying above it were approximately 100 unmolested German aeroplanes. The attacking Germans were supported by low-flying ground attack two-seaters from 16 *Schlachtstaffeln* (battle squadrons). These were protected by the ten *Jastas* of the two *Jagdgruppen*, while the airmen of JG III patrolled the higher airspace. The Germans held control of the air, and it was not until the evening that enemy aircraft were encountered. The only casualty in JG III was sustained when Alfred Hübner of *Jasta* 36 received a slight wound in the throat.

On 29 April, however, *Staffel* 36 would lose its inspiring leader when the daredevil Westphalian suffered a devastating wound. Bongartz had taken off on an afternoon patrol (apparently in pursuit of British bombers), but he soon returned to the aerodrome with a defective engine. He then departed in his reserve Dr I 575/17. Bongartz wrote the following melodramatic account some years later;

'During the Flanders battle in the spring of 1918 a large number of English bomber aeroplanes appeared above us just as my *Jagdstaffel* was having lunch. And then there was a dangerously close smashing, howling, and banging coming from our airfield, as though it were crying out in horror at the impact of every bomb tearing ridiculous holes in its beautiful turf.

'We spent little time wiping our mouths, and in the blink of an eye we were by our machines. "All clear?" the mechanic hastily asked, when one was sitting in the crate. "Clear!" was the answer, and with short tugs the propeller was thrown. The engine sprang to life. I took off from the field in front of the hangar, up and away, with the *Staffel* behind me.

'Unfortunately, we only caught one straggler from the English pack. The other bombers were no longer to be found. They were lucky, and for us it was a bad day. Heavy, low-lying

Jasta 27 leader Göring attained his 18th victory on 7 April. Here, Göring is seen in the cockpit of one of his Dr Is, likely 206/17. He had his aircraft equipped with sheet metal baffles that were fitted on the coaming just aft of the guide for the ammunition belt. These baffles were intended to deflect the empty cartridge cases that were ejected from the guns. This Dr I was also fitted with a rack of signal flare cartridges and a small ring sight on the right hand machine gun

clouds provided excellent cover for our foe, but for us made any sort of pursuit impossible. For a while we wandered around the sky between the tall white towers of cloud, whereby several times members of my *Staffel* were in danger of colliding. There was no point in flying around like that, and so with my hand I gave the *Staffel* the sign to return home. On a day like that one had to fly alone or at most in pairs. I therefore waved to my closer countryman, Paul Bäumer, and buzzed with him towards the front. There was a firm understanding between the two of us that when we were flying together one would attack and the other would provide protection.

'Above frozen trenches and craters Bäumer had quickly discovered an English infantry cooperation aeroplane circling at a low height, which was calmly patrolling along our lines amidst the smoke of exploding shells. He dove down upon him, with me trailing behind.

'However, after a few rounds, Bäumer eased off his opponent, in the meantime making a signal towards me, which I interpreted as jammed machine guns. It was a fateful mistake! In reality Bäumer had by chance discovered through a hole in the clouds a flight of enemy fighter aeroplanes that I could not see. Immediately after Bäumer's signal I therefore attacked the English infantry cooperation aeroplane without concern, and whispered a little saying about his ears from both guns. Despite the clattering and hammering of the motor and firing pins I suddenly noticed that I myself was being heavily fired upon. The situation was quickly grasped. Eight Englishmen were popping away at me, resulting in ricochets from the metal parts of the machine whistling about my nose in a nasty way. Afterwards it was determined, for example, that no fewer than 38 rounds had hit the engine housing alone.

'Bäumer, my faithful comrade, turned from a curve towards the Englishmen in order to take the heat off me. I too put my swift Fokker triplane into a sharp turn, as I wanted to get out of the enemy's field of fire. Then I felt a blow to my left temple, and at the same time experienced a burning sensation and flickering before my eyes. My goggles slid away. Glass splinters were stuck to my face. I could no longer see anything, and a hot stream of blood poured over my nose and mouth. Before I could come to a clear decision a crazy, indescribable pain tore my cranial nerves apart, causing me to scream horribly, and for a moment I almost lost consciousness. But the awareness of the great danger in which I found myself returned with alert senses. It overcame the piercing pain and all feelings of weakness. I had to, and wanted to, land at any price. "Lord help me!" And it was successful.

'I could not touch my left eye. I felt as though a draft were whistling through a hole in my forehead all the way to my brain, so that I could no longer breathe for all the torturous pain. However, with my glove I was able to free my right eye of blood, while on the left side I tried desperately to shut my eye in order to stem the stream of blood.

'All things considered, my last landing at the front was not bad at all. I set the machine down in a field of craters on Mount Kemmel without breaking anything or flipping over. Blood was flowing from my temple, my nose and my mouth. It had poured all over my leather vest and even my fur boots. Then there was this maddening pain. I had to pull myself together so that I didn't run away. An infantry officer came towards me from a command dugout. I introduced myself to him. *(Text continues on page 42.)*

This portrait photo of Heinrich Bongartz was taken during the first weeks of 1918 when he was home on his *Pour le Mérite* leave. On 29 April 1918 Bongartz suffered his final wound in combat against SE 5a fighters from No 74 Sqn. He received a bullet in the head that went through his left temple, eye and nose. He struggled to stave off unconsciousness long enough to bring Dr I 575/17 down safely in the shell-torn landscape near Mount Kemmel (*L Bronnenkant*)

COLOUR PLATES

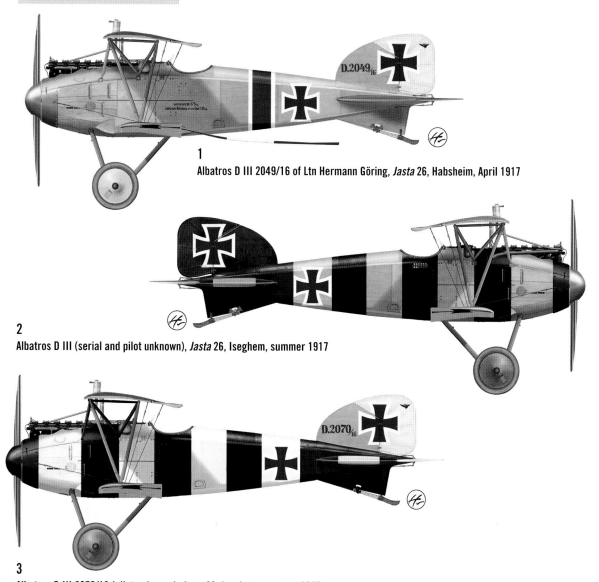

1
Albatros D III 2049/16 of Ltn Hermann Göring, *Jasta* 26, Habsheim, April 1917

2
Albatros D III (serial and pilot unknown), *Jasta* 26, Iseghem, summer 1917

3
Albatros D III 2070/16 (pilot unknown), *Jasta* 26, Iseghem, summer 1917

4
Albatros D V 1072/17 of Ltn d R Johannes Wintrath, *Jasta* 'Boelcke', Varsenaere, September 1917

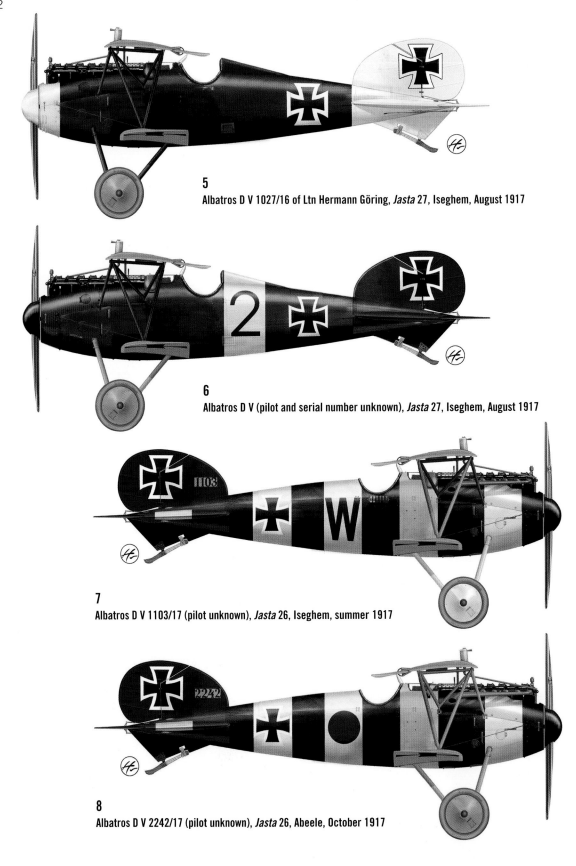

5
Albatros D V 1027/16 of Ltn Hermann Göring, *Jasta* 27, Iseghem, August 1917

6
Albatros D V (pilot and serial number unknown), *Jasta* 27, Iseghem, August 1917

7
Albatros D V 1103/17 (pilot unknown), *Jasta* 26, Iseghem, summer 1917

8
Albatros D V 2242/17 (pilot unknown), *Jasta* 26, Abeele, October 1917

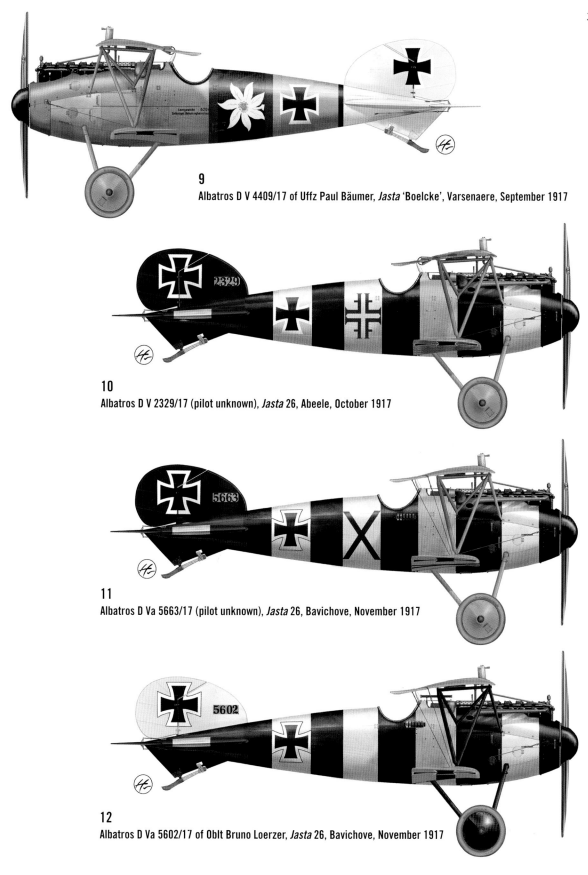

9
Albatros D V 4409/17 of Uffz Paul Bäumer, *Jasta* 'Boelcke', Varsenaere, September 1917

10
Albatros D V 2329/17 (pilot unknown), *Jasta* 26, Abeele, October 1917

11
Albatros D Va 5663/17 (pilot unknown), *Jasta* 26, Bavichove, November 1917

12
Albatros D Va 5602/17 of Oblt Bruno Loerzer, *Jasta* 26, Bavichove, November 1917

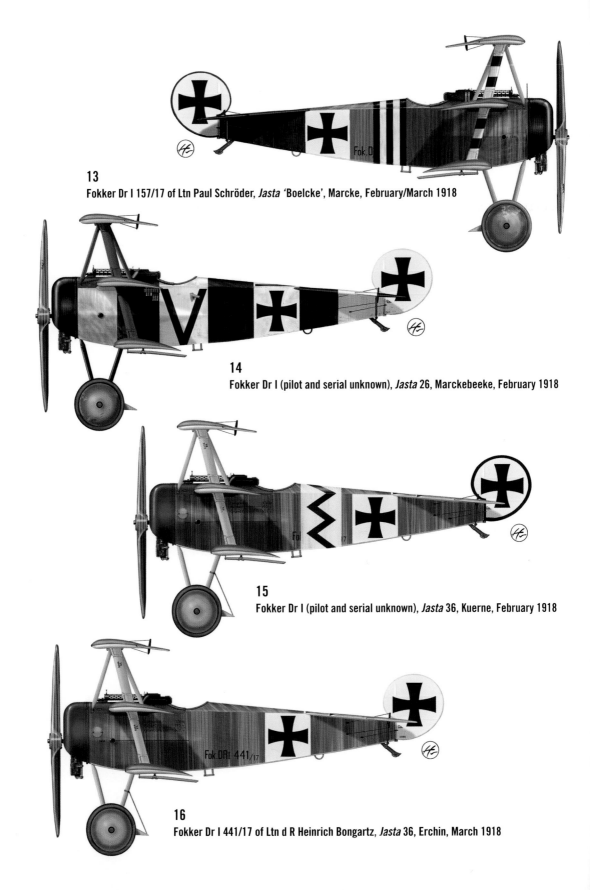

13
Fokker Dr I 157/17 of Ltn Paul Schröder, *Jasta* 'Boelcke', Marcke, February/March 1918

14
Fokker Dr I (pilot and serial unknown), *Jasta* 26, Marckebeeke, February 1918

15
Fokker Dr I (pilot and serial unknown), *Jasta* 36, Kuerne, February 1918

16
Fokker Dr I 441/17 of Ltn d R Heinrich Bongartz, *Jasta* 36, Erchin, March 1918

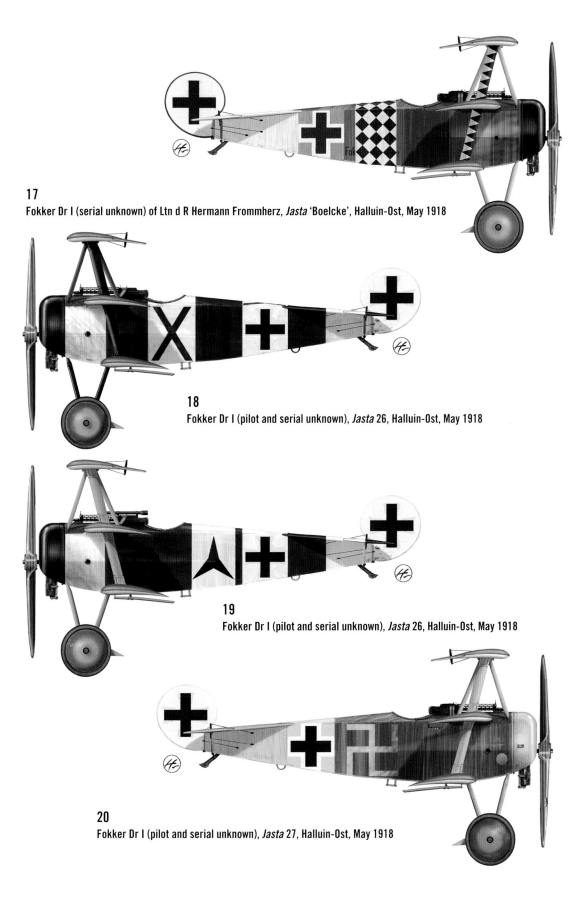

17
Fokker Dr I (serial unknown) of Ltn d R Hermann Frommherz, *Jasta* 'Boelcke', Halluin-Ost, May 1918

18
Fokker Dr I (pilot and serial unknown), *Jasta* 26, Halluin-Ost, May 1918

19
Fokker Dr I (pilot and serial unknown), *Jasta* 26, Halluin-Ost, May 1918

20
Fokker Dr I (pilot and serial unknown), *Jasta* 27, Halluin-Ost, May 1918

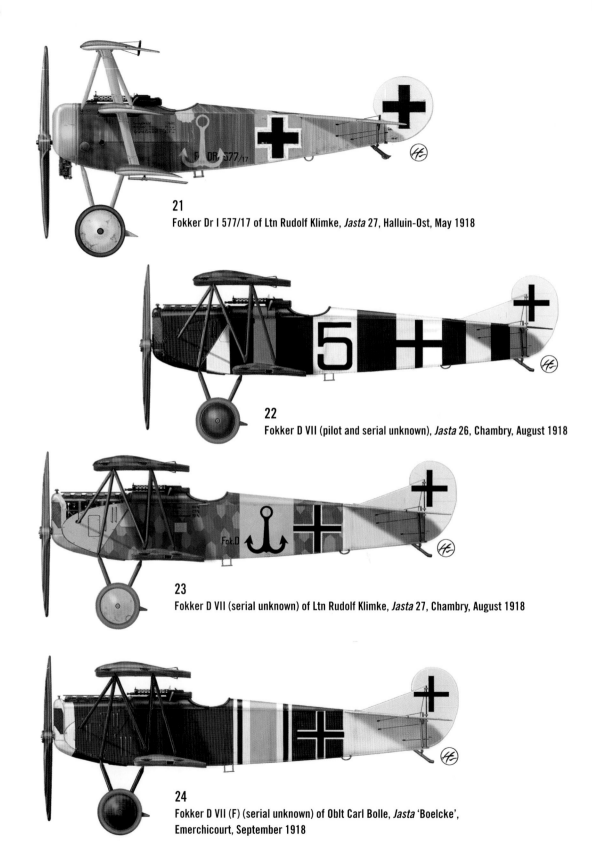

21
Fokker Dr I 577/17 of Ltn Rudolf Klimke, *Jasta* 27, Halluin-Ost, May 1918

22
Fokker D VII (pilot and serial unknown), *Jasta* 26, Chambry, August 1918

23
Fokker D VII (serial unknown) of Ltn Rudolf Klimke, *Jasta* 27, Chambry, August 1918

24
Fokker D VII (F) (serial unknown) of Oblt Carl Bolle, *Jasta* 'Boelcke',
Emerchicourt, September 1918

25
Fokker D VII (F) (pilot and serial unknown), *Jasta* 26, Lens, October 1918

26
Fokker D VII (F) 5109/18 of Ltn Alfred Lindenberger, *Jasta* 'Boelcke', Lens, October 1918

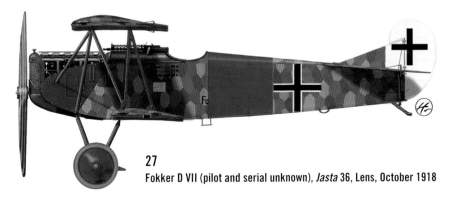

27
Fokker D VII (pilot and serial unknown), *Jasta* 36, Lens, October 1918

28
Fokker D VII (F) 4348/18 of Oblt Kurt von Griesheim(?), *Jasta* 'Boelcke', Lens, October 1918

38

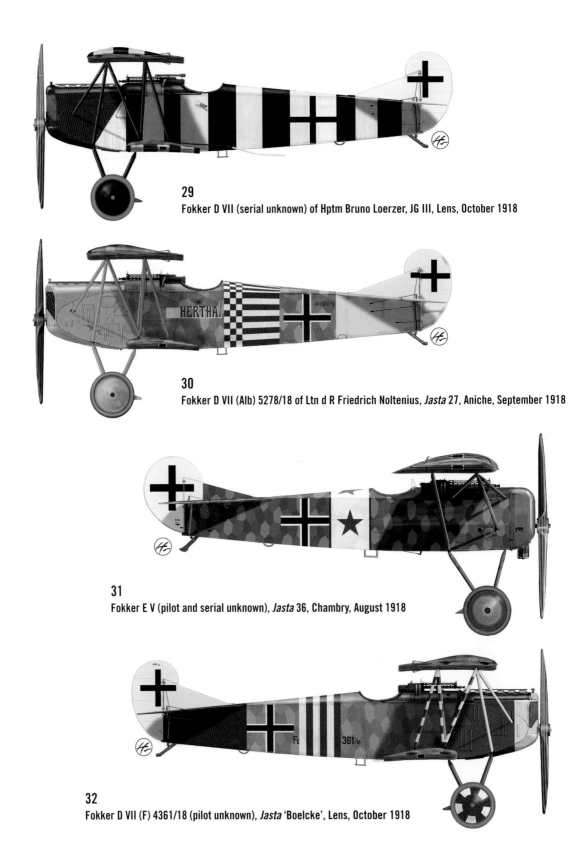

29
Fokker D VII (serial unknown) of Hptm Bruno Loerzer, JG III, Lens, October 1918

30
Fokker D VII (Alb) 5278/18 of Ltn d R Friedrich Noltenius, *Jasta* 27, Aniche, September 1918

31
Fokker E V (pilot and serial unknown), *Jasta* 36, Chambry, August 1918

32
Fokker D VII (F) 4361/18 (pilot unknown), *Jasta* 'Boelcke', Lens, October 1918

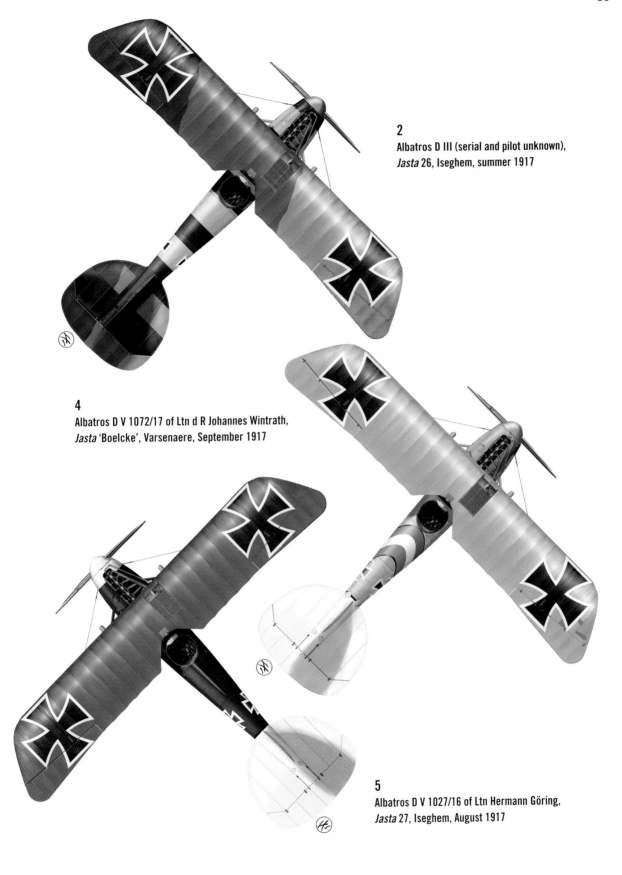

2
Albatros D III (serial and pilot unknown),
Jasta 26, Iseghem, summer 1917

4
Albatros D V 1072/17 of Ltn d R Johannes Wintrath,
Jasta 'Boelcke', Varsenaere, September 1917

5
Albatros D V 1027/16 of Ltn Hermann Göring,
Jasta 27, Iseghem, August 1917

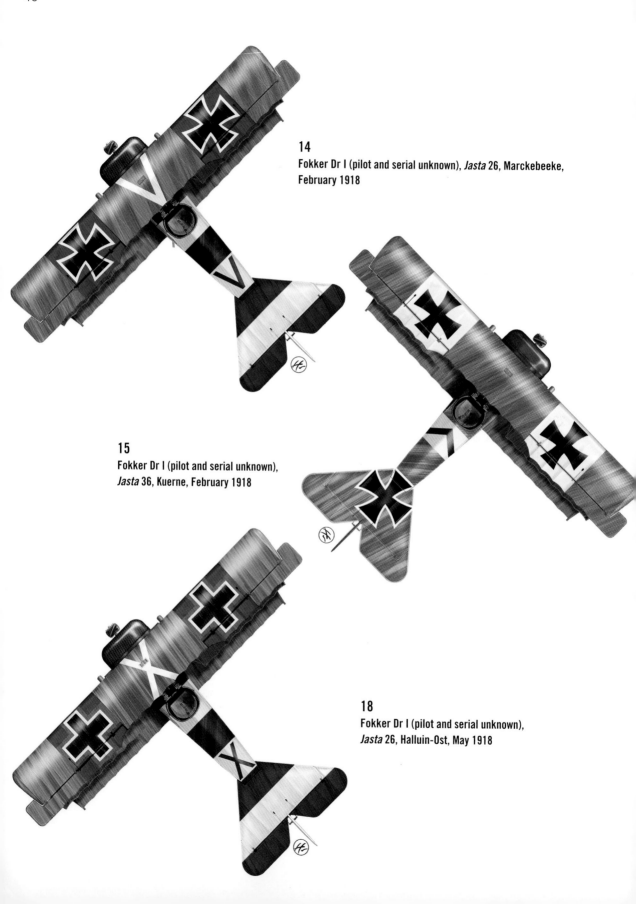

14
Fokker Dr I (pilot and serial unknown), *Jasta* 26, Marckebeeke, February 1918

15
Fokker Dr I (pilot and serial unknown), *Jasta* 36, Kuerne, February 1918

18
Fokker Dr I (pilot and serial unknown), *Jasta* 26, Halluin-Ost, May 1918

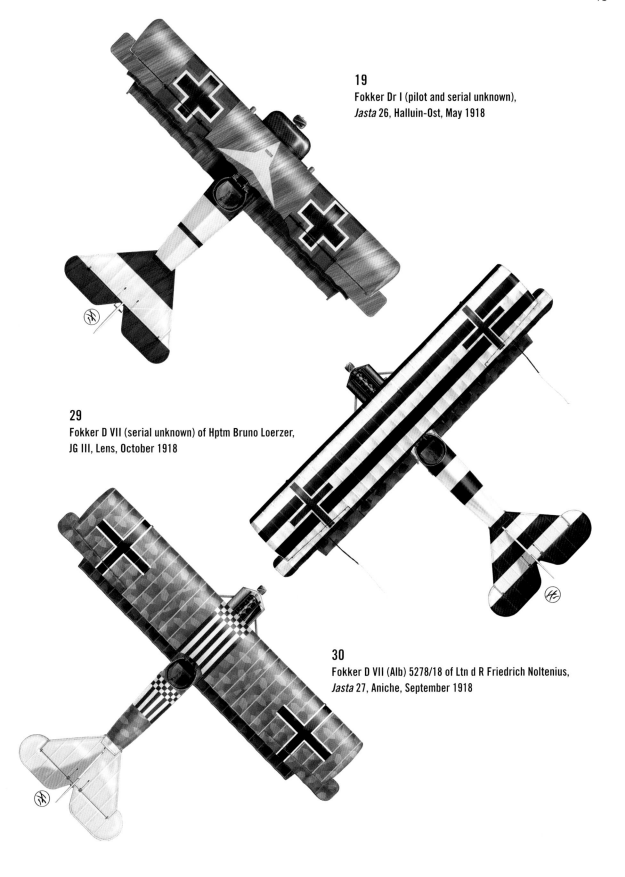

19
Fokker Dr I (pilot and serial unknown),
Jasta 26, Halluin-Ost, May 1918

29
Fokker D VII (serial unknown) of Hptm Bruno Loerzer,
JG III, Lens, October 1918

30
Fokker D VII (Alb) 5278/18 of Ltn d R Friedrich Noltenius,
Jasta 27, Aniche, September 1918

'"Oh woe", he lamented in my stead, as it were. "What do you have there on your face?"

'"Where?" I asked in reply, and noticed that something was dangling on my left cheek. I grabbed it and I myself tore off the eye which was hanging by a sinew from its smashed socket. That finished me off, and I collapsed unconscious in my machine. Only in the hospital train did I come back to my senses, and discovered that the nasty shot had passed through my temple, eye and nose on the left side.'

The infantry officer mentioned was probably the unnamed 'comrade' who wrote the following version of the incident – there are discrepancies in the two accounts, not surprising given the intense trauma that Bongartz suffered;

'This afternoon a Fokker triplane came down and flipped over. The pilot crawled out from under it covered in blood and with his eye shot out. He first walked around his aircraft, took a look at it, and then came towards us with his eye hanging down. He introduced himself with a bow, "Heinrich Bongartz".

'We bandaged him up, and I immediately ordered an auto. He was in terrible pain, as the round had passed through his temple and lodged in his nose, for which reason he could not get any air through his nose. In addition, he said, "*Ja, Ja*, we all take our turn!" A well-known English naval formation (sic) had surprised him in the clouds. The aeroplane was totally shot-up and spattered with blood. With this frightful wound he was still able to land and walk, but not for long. He received a morphine injection and then he lay quite still.'

Bongartz' Dr I 575/17 had, in fact, been attacked by an SE 5a formation from the redoubtable No 74 Sqn, led by high-scoring ace Capt 'Mick' Mannock himself. Besides Bäumer, there were other *Jasta* 'B' pilots in the area, and Ltn Ludwig Wortmann's triplane was shot down in flames by Mannock. Capt C B Glynn reported that his SE 5a and the leading Dr I (Bongartz) were firing head-on at each other just before he saw the Fokker dive vertically. Glynn received credit for the Dr I (although the *Jasta* 36 war diary stated that Bongartz was hit by a fighter behind him), and would go on to claim seven more victories and receive the DFC. Bongartz' war, however, was over. The *Jasta* 36 adjutant, Ltn d R Müller, took him to War Hospital No 661 at Roubaix. Bongartz would survive, having earned the dubious distinction of the Wound Badge in silver. On 30 April Ltn d R Plange from *Jasta* 'Boelcke', with seven victories, was transferred in as acting commander of *Staffel* 36.

By the end of April 1918 the advance of the ground forces had stopped as Operation *Georgette* lost its momentum. Uffz Ernst Messtorff of *Jasta* 26 was killed on 2 May (possibly by pilots from No 19 Sqn), but fine weather the next day allowed Carl Bolle of *Jasta* 'Boelcke' to destroy a No 73 Sqn Camel, as well as a DH 9

Although this is not Bongartz' crash-landed Dr I 575/17, this photo gives a glimpse of a similar situation. This blue-nosed *Jasta* 36 Dr I went through a forced landing, apparently flipping over and damaging the rudder. It has been righted, and *Staffel* mechanics have arrived to dismantle it

Jasta 26 triplane pilots decimated 'B' Flight of No 74 Sqn on 8 May 1918, recording four victories. Here, JG III commander Bruno Loerzer poses with his brother's *Staffel*. These pilots are, from left to right, Vzfw Erich Buder, Uffz Fritz Classen, Ltn d R Fritz Zogmann (at left in window), Vzfw Riemer, Ltn d R Weiss (OzbV, at right in window), Ltn d R Fritz Loerzer (CO), Oblt Bruno Loerzer, Ltn d R Otto Marquardt, Ltn d R Werner Dahm (left in window), Offz Stv Otto Esswein, Offz Stv Fritz Kublum (at right in window), Vzfw Otto Fruhner and (possibly) Vzfw Fritz Beckhardt

This photo of *Jasta* 26 triplanes being readied for flight was taken by a *Kogenluft* photographer during a visit to Halluin-Ost in May. The pilots' personal markings were applied to the white band just aft of the cockpit, and these were usually repeated on the top wing centre-section. The foremost Dr I, however, displayed a white '5' on the upper wing, with coloured bands on the fuselage. Otto Esswein's Dr I with his 'E' emblem is third in line. The fourth triplane was marked with a black 'Mercedes Star' on the fuselage, which was repeated in white on the top wing. The mechanics stand by to assist the pilots with their flying gear, which is seen on the ground at right

bomber from No 98 Sqn. *Jasta* 27 suffered the loss of one pilot on 7 May and another the following day.

The inferiority of their remaining Albatros fighters was more apparent than ever to the JG III pilots. Even their triplanes were proving a disappointment because of the unreliability of their rotary engines (due to poor-quality oil) and their slow speed. The pilots were eagerly anticipating re-equipping with new Fokker D VIIs that they heard were soon to arrive. Nonetheless, in the hands of the experienced pilots of JG III, well-handled triplanes could still be very potent adversaries – as was amply demonstrated on 8 May 1918.

That day JG III triplanes tangled with SE 5as from No 1 Sqn, and Bolle shot down one behind German lines south of St Eloi. In the same fight, Harry von Bülow of *Jasta* 36 brought down ten-victory ace and flight commander Capt C C Clark, who was taken prisoner slightly wounded, for his fourth success. At 1420 hrs *Jasta* 'Boelcke' encountered Camels from No 43 Sqn and Bolle and Ltn d R Friedrich 'Fritz' Kempf each shot one down – Kempf was flying Dr I 493/17 for this, his fourth victory. The best day, however, was had by *Jasta* 26.

That morning B and C Flights of No 74 Sqn were on a bombing flight to Menin, with C Flight (led by future high-scoring ace Capt J I T 'Taffy' Jones) about ten minutes behind B Flight. Five SE 5as from 'B' Flight, led by Capt W Young, had just dropped their bombs and were returning at about 5500 metres. They were unaware that they were being stalked by Fritz Loerzer and his *Kette* of *Jasta* 26 triplanes. Loerzer had cannily positioned his group 300 metres higher than 'B' Flight, carefully noting that 'C' Flight was still far too low and too far away to intervene. Loerzer duly led the black and white Fokkers down out of the sun on 'B' Flight. 'Taffy' Jones would write;

'The triplanes cut off the SEs over Gheluvelt, and the unequal contest started immediately. We could do nothing to help. Nothing! Within a minute of the start of the fight we saw an SE come hurtling down, smoking badly, before bursting into flames. It passed quite near me, but owing to the smoke I could not recognise the number on the nose. I know now it was poor old Stuart-Smith. A little later on, another SE passed down, burning fiercely. It was [Lt R E] Bright. By God, it was a grim sight! Then an SE came spinning through, with a tripe following. I made a dive after him. So did the others. The Hun, hearing the machine guns behind him, left the SE 5 and dived away east. The SE came out of the spin at about 2000 ft, then glided toward our lines. We saw him crash in the trenches. It was dear old Piggott.'

Of the five SE 5as of 'B' Flight, only one returned to the No 74 Sqn aerodrome at Clairmarais. Young's scout was so badly damaged that he had to land elsewhere, while Lt Piggott survived his crash landing. Lts P J Stuart-Smith and Bright were dead, however. Victories were awarded to *Jasta* 26 aces Fritz Classen, Erich Buder, Helmut Lange and Fritz Loerzer (his tenth).

Jasta 26 pilots don their flying clothing and prepare for a sortie. The Dr I at left displays the narrower chord form of cross that was more in line with the directive of 17 March, while the other two machines still bear the earlier, thicker style. Esswein's machine is in the centre, with the 'E' emblem on the wing mostly obscured by the cap of the foreground figure. The triplane at extreme right is the 'Mercedes Star'-marked machine

Jasta 'Boelcke's' ranks were bolstered on 9 May by the arrival of Ltn d R Alfred Lindenberger. The 21-year-old Stuttgart native already had three victories to his name after serving as an observer with *FA* 234(A) in 1917. Two of those were SPADs downed as he flew with Vzfw Kurt Jentsch as his pilot – Jentsch would also later fly in *Jasta* 'Boelcke'.

On 16 May 1918, *Jasta* 36's temporary commander, Ltn d R Richard Plange, was appointed permanent *Staffelführer*. His time in that position would be brief, however. Born on Christmas Eve 1892, he had joined *Jasta* 'Boelcke' on 7 September 1917 and then been wounded just two weeks later, spending a short time in hospital. After Plange's return in October he had been a steady, reliable performer, obtaining his first *Luftsieg* on 6 November and adding six more in the first four months of 1918.

On the morning of 19 May 1918, Plange was flying his Fokker Dr I 546/17 at the head of his *Jasta* 36 pilots near Zillebeke Lake when he sighted an Armstrong Whitworth FK 8 from No 10 Sqn doing artillery observation. The two-seater was crewed by Lt W Hughes and his observer, 2Lt F C Peacock MC. At about 1000 hrs German time, they saw two triplanes separate from their *Staffel* and dive straight for them. Peacock trained his twin Lewis guns on the leading Fokker and opened up. Despite the German's bullets hitting home around him, the observer kept firing and saw the triplane stagger away. It impacted behind the British lines, crashing southeast of Ypres. Plange was dead, and the shattered wreckage of his Dr I was given the British number 2/Bde/10.

THIRD BATTLE OF THE AISNE

Yet another JG III pilot had now died in a *Dreidecker*. Luckily, early examples of the Fokker D VII were now reaching the *Geschwader*, with *Jasta* 27 apparently being the first unit to receive a few of the outstanding biplane fighters. Once again, however, there were insufficient numbers available for the entire unit. *Staffel* 27, therefore, was forced to operate with a mix of three different types for a period – Albatros D Vas and Fokker Dr Is and D VIIs. New D VIIs also went to *Jastas* 'Boelcke' and 26. *Jasta* 36 would have to persevere with its old triplanes and do the best it could. The surplus triplanes from the other three *Jastas* were turned over to *AFP* 6 before JG III was transferred south to the 7th Army sector.

On 28 May 1918, Fritz Loerzer achieved his 11th victory. Loerzer's pilots of *Jasta* 26 posed with Göring's *Jasta* 27 in front of Esswein's Dr I for this group portrait. Identities, as provided by Rudolf Klimke to Alex Imrie, are (*Jasta* number in parentheses), left to right, Rudolf Stoltenhoff (27), Heinz Müller (27), Fritz Zogmann (26), Claus Riemer (26), Rudolf Klimke (27), Fritz Loerzer (26), Helmut Lange (26), Karl Riehm (OzbV, 27), unknown visiting officer, Franz Brandt (26), Hermann Göring (27), Otto Marquardt (26), unknown, unknown, Erich Buder (26), Fritz Classen (26), Willy Neuenhofen (26), Fritz Kublum (26) and Wilhelm Stein (27)

Oblt Göring of *Jasta* 27 was awarded the *Pour le Mérite* on the last day of May. By that time his *Staffel* had received some of the first Fokker biplanes supplied to JG III, as evidenced in this photo taken at Halluin-Ost. Most of these machines were probably marked with the unit's yellow noses and tails. At left is an aircraft displaying the streaked camouflage characteristic of early D VIIs. Next is an Albatros D Va, probably painted black, with chrome yellow nose and tail and a white rudder, then a Dr I marked with a swastika on the fuselage, with its leading edge degraded and obscured

From 21 to 24 May the *Geschwader* was busily occupied moving to Vivaise airfield, near Versigny (some ten kilometres northwest of Laon). This was in preparation for Operation *Blücher-Yorck,* generally known as the Third Battle of the Aisne. The offensive was focused on capturing the Chemin des Dames Ridge before American troops could arrive in France in significant strength. For the first time the pilots of JG III bid farewell to their customary 'sporting' foes of the RAF and would now face the French air service.

Jasta 'Boelcke's' leader, Carl Bolle, displayed a typical German prejudice toward French airmen when he wrote;

'At the end of May, *Jagdgeschwader Nr* III – and with it the "Boelcke" *Staffel* – was transferred to the area around Laon. For the time being they had exclusively Frenchmen as opponents who, with their well-known restraint in the air, made them difficult to catch. As a result of our rapid advances at Soissons and Fismes, where they had lost their airfields during the first days of the offensive on the Marne, the enemy's aerial activities were utterly meaningless. It took many unsuccessful patrols to even meet an opponent in the air or to force a dogfight, not to mention achieving a victory.'

27 May 1918 was the opening day of the offensive. That day also saw the appointment of Ltn d R Harry von Bülow-Bothkamp as commander of *Jasta* 36 – he thus followed in the footsteps of his late brother Walter.

Operation *Blücher-Yorck* began with a massive bombardment, with about two million shells being fired in just four hours. This was followed by a successful assault by 17 *Sturmtruppen* Divisions, the assault troops advancing an unprecedented 21 kilometres on the first day. The bridges on the Aisne were taken and the Germans continued their advance towards the Marne. On the battle's second day, *Jasta* 26's leader Fritz Loerzer scored the first *Geschwader* victory of the offensive when he forced down a SPAD at 1230 hrs for his 11th victory. On 29 May, as ground troops advanced south from the Chemin des Dames, Bolle shot up another SPAD near Fismes. Its pilot, however, was not a Frenchman but an American – Cpl Clarence Shoninger, serving in *Escadrille* SPA99. He was one of many 'Yanks' serving as volunteers in the French air service at that time, collectively known as the Lafayette Flying Corps (LFC). Shoninger's SPAD was riddled as Bolle's accurate fire severed the controls – it crashed alongside a flak battery near Crugny, and Shoninger survived as a wounded prisoner.

Bolle's victory was overshadowed by the temporary loss of one of the most proficient aces of his *Staffel* on the same day. Paul Bäumer had flown out at a rather late hour, perhaps to familiarise himself with the new region. He was returning to the aerodrome at Vivaise in near-darkness when he misjudged the landing approach and crashed. Bäumer suffered a severe fracture of his lower jaw and would take several months to recuperate – he would eventually return to combat in September and make up for lost time.

On 30 May the *Geschwader* commander, Bruno Loerzer, managed to leave his desk duties long enough to shoot up a SPAD for his 24th victory – his first in more than two months. He had probably brought down Cpl Robert Sarkis of SPA84, who was made a PoW. On that same day Fritz Classen of *Jasta 26* brought down one of the hardy Breguet 14 two-seaters at Souvy-Montgobert for his fourth claim. On the ground, the advancing troops reached Château Thierry. The Germans were now only 56 kilometres from Paris, but that was as far as they would get.

The fifth day of the offensive (31 May) was an active one for JG III, and especially *Jasta 26*. In just 15 minutes between 1705 hrs and 1720 hrs, three of its pilots were credited with four SPADs downed in the area around Montfortaine and the Forest of Compiégne. Two were claimed by Esswein, and one each by Lange and Vzfw Christian Mesch. One hour later Oblt Maximilian von Förster of *Jasta* 27 put in his own claim for a SPAD. Although he was apparently denied this claim by *Kogenluft, Jasta* 27 still recorded it as its 51st victory. Two *Jasta* 'B' pilots recorded attacks on Breguets. Ltn Alfred Lindenberger's claim was later confirmed as his fifth victory, but Ltn d R Ernst Bormann received only a 'forced to land' notation for his, since his opponent landed at Teille, near Laon, in French lines. Uffz Heinrich Koch of *Jasta* 36 also attacked a two-seater, but he was killed when his Dr I had its rudder controls shot away by the French observer and the triplane crashed near Soissons.

Certainly the biggest news at *Jasta* 27 on 31 May was the announcement of the award of Göring's *Pour le Mérite*. There has been much discussion by historians about the unusual circumstances surrounding the bestowal of the 'Blue Max' to Göring at this point in his career. At this time the usual benchmark for the award of the *Pour le Mérite* to a *Jagdflieger* was at least 20 victories – Göring only had 18. Ambitious to the utmost, the *Jasta* 27 leader had long lobbied his superiors for this and other awards. Göring had astutely ingratiated himself with *Kofl* 4 Hptm Wilberg and *Kogenluft* von Hoeppner, as well as Crown Prince Wilhelm, who was nominally in command of the Army Group that included the 7th Army.

The month of June opened with Alfred Lindenberger sending another Breguet down near Priez – his second in two days. However, his Breguet of 31 May was recorded as his fifth

Staffelführer Bolle of *Jasta* 'B' was credited with a SPAD downed near Dampleux on 3 June 1918. Bolle's Fokker Dr I 413/17 is seen here, marked with his usual fuselage bands in the yellow colour of his old cuirassier regiment, flanked by Prussian black and white bands. The black cowling with the white faceplate was part of the unit identification of *Jasta* 'B'

victory due to a delay in confirmation, while his 1 June opponent was confirmed as his fourth. Also on 1 June *Jasta* 27 lost Vzfw Wilhelm Stein, killed near Soissons, but the unit's Ltn d R Helmuth Roer downed a French aircraft at Château-Thierry. Fighting on 2 June resulted in another Breguet being downed by *Jasta* 'B', this time credited to Ltn d R Johannes Heemsoth for his first victory, and a SPAD VII fell to *Jasta* 36's Alfred Hübner for the second of his six successes. Hübner's opponent was probably Capt Maurice Rebreget of SPA62, killed on this day.

On 3 June the stunning advance made by the assault troops came to a standstill, as they were beset by supply shortages, fatigue, few reserves and heavy casualties. In the air, however, JG III had better luck. NCO pilot Fritz Kublum of *Jasta* 26 claimed a Breguet for his one and only success, Bolle shot down a SPAD at Fauborg to record his 13th victory and his *Jasta* 'B' comrade Hermann Frommherz got another one at Ancienville. Frommherz had returned to the *Staffel* from *Fliegerschule* 'Lübeck' on 18 May. The SPAD was only his third confirmed victim, but there would be no stopping him in the weeks ahead. Bolle, too, was clearly in good form, and he claimed a Breguet at Fresnes the following day for his 14th *Luftsieg.*

The advances achieved in the offensive forced JG III to resume its nomadic ways. On 3 June *Jasta* 27 moved to a meadow at Mont de Soissons Ferme (a former French airfield), where it was joined by *Jasta* 'Boelcke' three days later and by *Jasta* 26 on the 8th – *Jasta* 36 had set up facilities at Epitaphe Ferme 48 hours earlier. Three of the *Staffeln* in JG III were now fully equipped with D VIIs, *Jastas* 'Boelcke', 26 and 27 having given up most of their triplanes to *AFP* 7, perhaps retaining only a few as reserve machines. *Jasta* 36, however, would keep its Dr Is much longer.

Göring was the first to score from the new location, on 5 June, whilst leading four other *Jasta* 27 airmen in his D VII 278/18, identified by his usual markings of a white nose and tail. The report requesting confirmation of his 19th victory read as follows;

'On 5/6/18 at about 1000 hrs, I dived with my *Staffel* over the northern part of the forest of Villers-Cotterêts on French aircraft that were conducting an artillery shoot. They flew away to the west. I overtook a two-seater (A.R.) and shot it down at 1100 metres – it crashed in the crossroads just east of Vivieres, 240 rounds fired. The remaining French were chased to the west by the *Staffel.* As I circled over the crash site, I was fired on by flak.'

Although Göring identified his victim as an AR type, it was more likely a Breguet.

Göring also supplied the next victory for the *Geschwader*, recorded as his 20th and the 52nd for *Jasta* 27 on 9 June. This time he was flying D VII 324/18, which also bore his white tail and engine cowling markings. Göring wrote;

'On 9/6/18 at about 0845 hrs, I dived, with my *Staffel,* on a SPAD that was flying low over our frontlines. From an altitude of 400 metres, he dropped straight down like a stone and hit at the northwest corner of Horseshoe Wood south of Corey, behind out frontlines. I circled several times over the crash site. 200 rounds fired.'

Cpl Pierre Chan of SPA94 was captured. One of Göring's pilots, Vzfw Wilhelm 'Willy' Neuenhofen, also shot down a SPAD for his all-important first victory that same day.

9 June 1918 was also the opening day of Ludendorff's fourth offensive, known as Operation *Gneisenau*, or the Battle of the Matz to the Allies. The goal was to eliminate a salient extending into the German lines. The 18th Army was to attack in the north toward Compiègne on the 9th, and the following day the 7th Army would advance from the south to capture Villers-Cotterêts. For this attack JG III was ordered to coordinate with the 'Richthofen' *Geschwader* as noted in the JG I war diary;

'Together with *Jagdgeschwader Nr* III, the *Geschwader* undertook the protection of the 18th Army's flank in the Noyon-Compiègne-Vic sur Aisne sector. Attack went well.'

The new Fokker biplanes were proving very effective, but they did not always guarantee success. On 12 June Fritz Loerzer's D VII crash-landed behind the French lines about 11 kilometres southwest of Soissons, near Cutry. He later stated that the Fokker's rudder controls failed during combat as he pursued a French opponent. It is not clear if this was due to enemy fire or not. For four long, anxious, weeks, his brother Bruno had no news of Fritz. Then, finally, a report came through from the French that he was a prisoner. In the meantime, *Jasta* 26's Ltn d R Bollmann assumed temporary command of the unit until 27 June, when five-victory ace Ltn d R Franz Brandt transferred in from *Jasta* 27 to take over.

On 13 June, with his missing brother still in his thoughts, Bruno Loerzer led *Jasta* 26 into battle himself and shot down a SPAD over Dommiers at 1920 hrs. The fighter may have been a machine from SPA100 flown by Brig Maxime Ouizille, who was captured. Two other *Jasta* 26 pilots in this combat, Vzfw Christian 'Christel' Mesch and Vzfw Fritz Classen, also claimed SPADs, although Classen's remained unconfirmed. Another SPAD fell to the guns of Ltn Kurt Jacob of *Staffel* 36, and he added a French balloon at Retheuil to bring his score to three.

On 14 June Carl Bolle – now promoted to Oberleutnant – shot down a Breguet 14B2 west of Laversine for his 15th victory and the 227th for the *Staffel*. It seems likely that this was a bomber from BR29, flown by American 1Lt Robert Moore, with Lt Giquel as observer. This crew was attacked by fighters behind German lines at an altitude of 4800 metres. In their first pass, the fighters' fire killed the observer, whose body fell on the controls and jammed them. The bomber plummeted down, with Moore struggling to regain control as two pursuers poured an 'incessant fire into his machine'. Slowly, Moore regained some control, although he was wounded three times in the arm and right side as the Fokkers chased him down to 1000 metres. Nevertheless, he managed to land his riddled aeroplane, subsequently recovering in a French hospital.

During the evening of the 15th Willy Neuenhofen of *Jasta* 27 downed a SPAD for his second confirmed kill. Neuenhofen was a Westphalian, born in

On 17 June Rudolf Klimke was one of three *Jasta* 27 pilots to down French SPADs. This photo of Klimke was taken the previous month at Halluin-Ost, and it shows him in his well-worn Dr I 577/17. The *Staffel* markings of a yellow cowling, struts, rear fuselage and tail were no doubt applied to the aircraft. Klimke's personal emblem of an anchor was painted on the fuselage (barely visible) in yellow and on top of the tailplane in black. The anchor was applied at the behest of his mother, who believed it represented good hope – the virtue of hope is often portrayed as an anchor in Christian symbolism

München-Gladbach on 24 April 1897. On 1 July 1915 he reported to *FEA* 7 and flew as an NCO pilot with *FA* 215(A) on the Eastern Front through to 25 November 1917, when he was sent to *Jastaschule* I. From there Neuenhofen went to Westphalian *KEST* 8 from 9 to 30 December. On the last day of 1917 he was posted to *Jasta* 27, where he would really perform once equipped with the D VII.

Sunday, 16 June 1918 was a busy day for *Jasta* 'B' as Bolle, Heemsoth and Ltn d R Suer each chalked up a 'DH' claim – No 103 Sqn lost two DH 9s. The next day brought a mix of success and tragedy to JG III. In the morning, *Jastas* 26 and 27 engaged several SPADs, and *Staffel* 26 leader Franz Brandt brought down one of them. Göring, Klimke and three others from *Jasta* 27 attacked aircraft from SPA93, the former, who was again flying D VII 278/18, reporting;

'About 0830 hrs I spotted five SPADs attacking our captive balloons west of Soissons. With my *Staffel*, I came down and attacked them. During the course of the fight, from 500 metres, I downed a 200 hp SPAD that crashed at the western edge of the small woods of the Ambleny Heights. I saw, closely below me, Ltn Brandt force down a second SPAD. At the same moment, two of my Fokkers collided and crashed. Due to our attack, the German balloons remained unharmed.'

The unfortunates from *Jasta* 27 were Oblt von Förster and Vzfw Wilhelm Schäffer, both of whom were killed. Göring had forced a SPAD down in German territory for his 21st victory, as did Klimke for his ninth. SPA93 lost two pilots taken prisoner and SPA162 lost another, corresponding to the JG III claims. On 17 June Ltn d R Rudolf Stoltenhoff was posted back to *Jasta* 27 from *Jasta* 50 – he had previously flown with *Staffel* 27 from July 1917 to May 1918.

The frenetic pace of combat continued, with *Geschwader* commander Loerzer sustaining a light wound on 20 June. It was not serious, and he remained at the front. Four days later a Breguet fell to the consistently lethal aim of Carl Bolle, while *Jasta* 36's rising star Kurt Jacob shot down a SPAD south of Château-Thierry for his fourth victim. On 28 June Bolle brought down a SPAD to take his tally to 19.

Towards the end of June both Loerzer and Göring were called away to attend the second fighter aircraft type tests held at Adlershof airfield in Berlin, the home of the *Flugzeugmeisterei* (aircraft test establishment). These fighter trials were held so that experienced frontline *Jagdflieger* could assess new prototypes and recommend their choices for production.

On 3 July Göring had flown the new all-metal Zeppelin-Lindau D I (or Dornier D I) with duralumin stressed skin covering the cantilever wings and the fuselage. After wringing out the radical new machine, Göring landed and handed it over to Hptm Wilhelm Reinhard, who had taken command JG I after von Richthofen's death. As Reinhard dove from 1000 metres the D I's centre section struts broke and the top wing ripped away – Reinhard was killed in the ensuing crash. In a momentous turn of events, Oblt Hermann Göring was appointed commander of JG I on 8 July 1918. He now left JG III and his command of *Jasta* 27, Ltn d R Stoltenhoff being named acting commander in his place. Göring, of course, would ride his reputation as the 'last commander of the "Richthofen" *Geschwader*' to high political rank and eternal infamy.

JG III MEETS THE YANKS

On 28 June the 1st Pursuit Group of the fledgling US Air Service (USAS) had moved from the Toul sector to Touquin, some 32 kilometres south of Château-Thierry. While the group had compiled a respectable record thus far against Albatros and Pfalz pilots, the four Nieuport 28 squadrons of the 1st would now face more high calibre opposition – especially from JGs I and III. In a letter from this time, Lt John Mitchell of the 95th Aero Squadron wrote;

'They have several very fine squadrons opposite us. The very best the Germans ever had – every one of the pilots is an old hand. They surely know how to handle a machine.'

As usual, Mitchell and others believed that any top-quality opposition they encountered was from the 'Richthofen Circus', when in fact it was just as often JG III. The distinctive black and white banded D VIIs of *Jasta* 26 left a vivid impression on many Yanks and their Allies. According to German historian Ernst Schäffer, the aircraft of *Jasta* 26 were called the 'black and white squadron' by the British, and '*Les Damiers*' (the chequerboards) by the French. The broad black/white panels on the flat-sided Fokker fuselages gave many Americans an impression of a dreaded 'checkerboard circus' as well.

On 5 July Nieuports of the 95th Aero Squadron clashed with the Fokkers of *Jasta* 'Boelcke' – the new D VII types were still unfamiliar to the Yanks. 1Lt Waldo Heinrichs wrote in his diary;

'First big fight. Flew above another Nieuport patrol of four aeroplanes but got separated from them toward last. Ran into patrol of five or six Albatros D-5 (*sic*). We engaged with slight advantage of numbers. We mixed at once. One guy shot at me fully four times. He went down and I went up for one on my back. He out climbed and [out] speeded me. Thompson did not return. A Nieuport went down in flames.'

In this deadly melee it seems likely that Hermann Frommherz killed 1Lt S Thompson, while Bolle may have forced 1Lt C Rhodes down to be taken prisoner. On the succeeding day, Heinrichs reported another encounter with enemy fighters, but 'It was the famous checkered squadron that attacked this time and left us at once'.

On 7 July, a patrol of 11 Nieuports from Capt Eddie Rickenbacker's 94th Aero Squadron was busy assailing a pair of Rumpler *biplace* (two-seat) machines when some Fokkers from *Jasta* 26 intervened. 1Lt Cates reported, 'At 1000 hrs [a] Fokker *piqued* [dived] on me from the side, forcing me down to 800 meters'. 1Lt Hamilton Coolidge wrote, 'I left the battle pursued by a group of Fokker *monoplace* [single-seat] fighters who had come up in the meantime'. The Nieuport 28 N6181 of 1Lt William Chalmers was forced down intact and he was captured – credit for Nieuports was given to Franz Brandt, Erich Buder and Otto Fruhner of *Staffel* 26. Clearly, this was a case of over-claiming, but such optimistic claims were endemic on both sides in the hectic dogfights of the era.

The USAS's 94th Aero Squadron encountered *Jasta* 26 on 7 July 1918 and 1Lt William Chalmers was taken prisoner after his Nieuport 28 N6181 'white 15' was forced down. Three *Staffel* 26 pilots – Brandt, Buder and Fruhner – were each credited with a Nieuport, although only Chalmers was lost

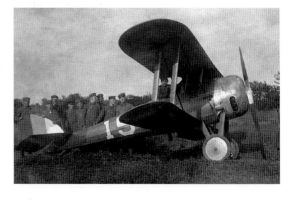

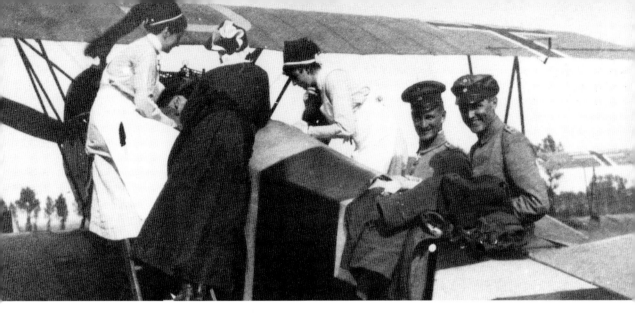

CHAPTER THREE

THE TIDE TURNS

On 20 July 1918 Bruno Loerzer achieved his 28th victory, but not without some argument from *Jasta* 27's leader, Rudolf Stoltenhoff, who also claimed the French SPAD. Here, Oblt Loerzer and his adjutant Oblt Theodor Dahlmann (at right) are entertaining some visiting nurses by giving them a look at a *Jasta* 26 D VII (*A Weaver*)

On 15 July 1918 the last of the Ludendorff drives was launched. Codenamed Operation *Friedensturm* (Peace Offensive), it became known as the Second Battle of the Marne to the Allies. The German 1st and 7th Armies would spearhead the attack, supported by the 3rd Army on the left flank and the 9th Army on the right. As a component of the 7th Army, JG III was in the thick of the fighting, reinforced by the 'closest possible cooperation' with JG I. They would face not only French and American squadrons but also British units, for the RAF had agreed to extend its offensive patrols southward to assist the hard-pressed French. However, the airmen of JG III were by now largely equipped with D VIIs, and the combination of these superb aircraft and newly issued parachutes (not trusted by all) bolstered their confidence.

Fortunately for JG III, it was at this crucial time that a talented newcomer joined *Jasta* 27. Ltn d R Friedrich Noltenius would prove to be a *Jagdflieger* of exceptional ability, and a talented writer. He kept a perceptive diary, which he copied and transcribed for Luftwaffe historians in 1936 – the diary was in turn translated into English by historian A E Ferko in the mid-1960s. It reveals that Noltenius possessed superb situational awareness and a great sense of how to plan an attack with the greatest advantage. However, he would also suffer a good deal of bad luck in regard to confirmations.

Friedrich Noltenius was born in the old Hanseatic League city of Bremen on 8 January 1894. His father was a professor of medicine and Friedrich was engaged in his own pre-med studies when the war broke out. On 4 August 1914 he voluntarily enlisted in *Feld-Artillerie-Regt König Karl (Württembergisches) Nr* 13. Noltenius served as an artillerist on both Eastern and Western Fronts, rising to the rank of Leutnant der Reserve. In 1917 he requested a transfer to aviation and was posted to *FEA* 1 in Altenburg on 3 November. Noltenius breezed through the studies there and proceeded on to *FEA* 10 in Böblingen for flight training. By early June he was a fully qualified pilot and was posted to *AFP* 7, then on to *FA* 234(A) for artillery-spotting duties. Noltenius spent only a week there before attending *Jastaschule* II in Nivelles – he joined *Staffel* 27 just before the offensive opened.

15 July was a day of high temperatures and rainstorms, but there was a tremendous amount of aerial activity, nevertheless. Some 225 French bombers dropped 40 tons of bombs on the pontoon bridges thrown over the Marne by the advancing Germans. The *Geschwader* pilots' part in the assault began early in the day, as Noltenius wrote;

'First day of the offensive on the Marne and Rheims front. We had orders to be ready for takeoff at 0600 hrs from our advanced landing field at Redly Ferme. A large bank of clouds approached from the west. We took off and climbed, circling above the cloud level.'

Noltenius wrote that *Jasta* leader Ltn d R Rudolf Stoltenhoff led them in a blind dive down through the thick cloud layer. They emerged beneath the overcast at 300 metres and were subjected to heavy fire from machine guns and rifles. Aside from that, the patrol was uneventful.

Jasta 26 was aloft at midday, and at 1255 hrs it pounced on a Breguet 14B2 – Erich Buder was credited with downing the aeroplane for his fourth victory. It was apparently a BR117 machine flown by American LFC pilot 1Lt Mandersohn Lehr, with observer Sous-Lt Carles. This crew had just dropped their bombs on the Marne bridges. In a heavy rainstorm, Lehr became separated from the other two aeroplanes in his flight and then ten enemy fighters attacked. The Breguet's motor was hit and Lehr received a mortal head wound. His observer succeeded in gaining some control of the burning aircraft and crossed the lines. In their vital book *The Lafayette Flying Corps,* author-pilots Nordhoff and Hall reported that, 'On landing, the machine turned over, the observer was thrown out and Lehr, who by this time was dead, found a funeral pyre in the flaming wreck of his Breguet'.

About 45 minutes later five pilots of *Jasta* 'B' engaged Camels from No 43 Sqn over Soilly. Once again Bolle proved the deadliest sharpshooter, destroying the Sopwith of 2Lt Babbitt, who fell near Dormans. Harry von Bülow was credited with a Nieuport 28 at the same spot, downed at 1410 hrs, while his *Jasta* 36 comrade Kurt Jacob received confirmation for an SE 5a five minutes later. Bülow's Nieuport opponent was from the 147th Aero Squadron, 2Lt T 'Abe' Abernethy having already fired at a 'black and white checkered bird' that he claimed as a 'probable' when five Fokkers from a different group dived on him.

Ltn d R Friedrich Noltenius was posted to *Jasta* 27 on 15 July 1918. He would prove a brilliant fighter pilot, with an analytical approach to attacking balloons. After the war he became an otolaryngologist, moving to South America in 1923. There, he earned the International Red Cross' 'Cross of Honour' for his service to mankind, before returning to Germany with his family in 1933. Noltenius was commissioned in the medical branch of the Luftwaffe, resumed flying and researched the new field of aero medicine. On 12 March 1936 he died when the Bücker Jungmann he was piloting crashed on takeoff

On 16 July JG III commander Bruno Loerzer shot down the 27th Aero Squadron Nieuport 28 of 1Lt Robert Raymond. This classic view illustrates one of Loerzer's highly decorated Fokker D VIIs. The black/white stripes of *Jasta* 26 were extended to the uppersurface of the top wing and the undersurface of the lower wing, thus making the *Geschwaderführer's* machine very distinctive so as to facilitate his leadership of large formations. This D VII was fitted with an Oigee telescopic sight, and a flare pistol protruded through the port side of the cockpit

After some furious scrapping, Abernethy found himself gliding for home with a dead engine, pursued by two of the D VIIs. 'I could smell those tracers going past my nose', he recalled many years later, 'and I had one pass through the sleeve of my flying suit and another dented the varnish on the fabric of the cowling just behind my head'. Abernethy, nonetheless, managed to cross the Marne and land safely in territory that had just been taken by US troops. His squadronmate 2Lt G A S Robertson was also chased deep into Allied lines by Fokkers before making a forced landing, and was apparently recorded as the sixth victory for Frommherz of *Jasta* 'B'.

Kurt Jacob had scored once, but he was not done for the day. Flying again late in the afternoon (1735 hrs), he attacked one of several large Caudron R XI escort fighters from *Escadrille* C46 that were protecting Breguet bombers targeting the Marne bridges. These formidable twin-engine aircraft featured a three-man crew that consisted of a pilot and two gunners. Jacob shot up the Caudron flown by Sgt Glenn Sitterly (another member of the LFC), with American Soldat William Mackerness and French Sgt-Maj Henry Lacassagne as gunners. Jacob's Spandaus set the big aircraft afire, but 'by a miracle' Sitterly brought it down in French lines near Villers-Cotterêts and the crew escaped serious injury.

The final victory of the day went to Uffz Reinhold Neumann from *Staffel* 36, who claimed a SPAD for his only confirmed success. 15 July had proven to be a highly productive day for JG III, with seven confirmed triumphs and only one pilot – Alfred Hübner of *Jasta* 36 – slightly wounded.

The offensive's second day, 16 July, was one of sunny, very hot weather and extremely mixed fortunes for the *Geschwader*. Noltenius flew four sorties that day and wrote, 'At the front things were really buzzing'. At 1410 hrs Erich Buder from *Jasta* 26 scored his 13th victory – a SPAD southwest of Igny. About 90 minutes later Oblt Loerzer shot down the Nieuport 28 of the 27th Aero Squadron's 1Lt Raymond DSC, who was taken prisoner. However, the high temperatures were a deadly problem for the second day running. 'Because of the extreme heat, the phosphorus ammunition ignited on its own', wrote Noltenius (this had resulted in the death of *Jasta* 10 ace Fritz Friedrichs the previous day). 'This cause was responsible for the loss of seven machines within the 7th Army. I heard of two parachute jumps from burning machines'.

At 1750 hrs Vzfw Gustav Nolte of *Jasta* 36 was mortally wounded, although he still had enough strength to take to his parachute. 'I saw a triplane attacking several two-seaters', wrote Noltenius. 'A short while later I saw a bundle drop from the German aeroplane, and the parachute softly brought our dead pilot down to earth – he had been shot through the heart. Esswein of *Jasta* 26 was luckier, however [he was downed after attacking a balloon and jumped at about the same time as Nolte]. He landed safely after having his fur boots pulled off while still in the air.'

The 17th was a day of heavy rains and fog that limited aerial action, and Noltenius recorded that the offensive on the ground had stagnated. The French had been joined by 85,000 American troops and the British XXII Corps, and the German advance was halted.

This failure to break through the Allied Armies allowed Commander-in-Chief Ferdinand Foch to launch his planned counteroffensive against the German salient on the 18th. Noltenius wrote, 'Along the frontline from Soissons to Château-Thierry [there is] heavy drum fire announcing a French counterattack'. Later in the day *Jasta* commander Stoltenhoff led Noltenius and others on a patrol;

'Against strong winds we flew in the direction of Soissons. We climbed and climbed to approximately 4500 metres. The cold air at this height made me a bit tired so that I was not sufficiently on my guard. Suddenly, the leader dived, and at the same moment I saw an enemy aircraft [a Breguet] spin down at my port side. I at once attacked him from a frontal position, forcing him to turn away. Three of our machines circled about the Frenchman, firing from time to time.

'Alternately, I was over or under him and behind him. Soon, the French observer ceased firing and I saw his guns pointing upwards. Unfortunately, I did not realise that the pilot must have been dead, as the machine no longer flew properly. Anyway, at an altitude of 2500 metres I took good aim and pressed the trigger. Then a body broke free of the seat and the observer fell out. It was an abominable sight, and I can only say that I was extremely sorry for the poor devil – the more so, as it would not have been necessary, because our *Staffelführer* told me [later] that the Frenchman had stuck up his arms, indicating surrender. We followed the machine until it crashed to the ground in the vicinity of Soissons.'

Noltenius was denied confirmation for this victory, while Neuenhofen was credited with a Breguet for his third score. 'Meanwhile, the situation at the front has changed severely', Noltenious continued. 'The Frenchmen had made considerable progress and we had to give up our airfields'. Although the German troops were in retreat, Bolle was still able to bring his own tally to 24 with a Breguet and a SPAD destroyed. These successes were offset by the loss of Kurt Jacob of *Jasta* 36. With a score of seven victories, he was wounded but landed safely at his home airfield and went to hospital.

The tide of the battle had turned, and from now on JG III would be in a steady state of retreat. On 19 July Noltenius wrote that by the end of the day the *Geschwader* had settled in at the new field at Vauxcére, but that the officers' mess was 'still in a rather bad condition'. The following day he reported;

'First takeoff at 0930 hrs, with *Staffel* 27 as top cover for *Staffel* 26. I was considerably lower than Stoltenhoff and Oblt [Bruno] Loerzer [flying with *Jasta* 26], and that is the reason for my not noticing an attack that they launched against an enemy formation. Suddenly, a spinning SPAD, which had been attacked by one of them, passed by. After the flight, there was great discussion as to who had been the one that shot it down.'

In the competitive world of the *Jagdflieger* there were no shared victories, and bitter arguments between rival claimants for the same victim were common. In this case, *Geschwader Kommandeur* Loerzer won out over Stoltenhoff and gained credit for the SPAD XIII – it was probably flown by Lt G Mazimann, the CO of SPA159, who was killed. Buder of *Jasta* 26 also destroyed a SPAD this day to 'make ace'.

That evening Noltenius took off with a *Jasta* 27 patrol that became embroiled in a fight with Nieuport 28s from the American 27th Aero Squadron. 'Neuenhofen had been attacked by three opponents', wrote Noltenius. 'He had caught one and shot him down, or rather, he forced him down. I saw Klimke following a machine, and with no other opponent in sight, I joined them. To judge from the pennant on his empennage, this must have been the leader of the enemy squadron. We forced him down. Once, attacking him from the side, I was a bit clumsy and absent-minded and he quickly pulled up and fired at me. Afterwards, I found two hits in my machine. The Nieuport (that was its make) prepared for a landing, but somersaulted in the process. The result of the first encounter, for me, with a single-seater *Staffel* – six of them (sic) attacked us five and two of them were shot down.'

Klimke and Neuenhofen each gained credit for one of the Nieuports. From the flight of five USAS pilots, Lt Zenos Miller was captured, 2Lt John MacArthur fell behind German lines badly wounded and died as a prisoner on 9 August and Lt Fred Norton DSC was hit in the chest and right arm, but still brought his Nieuport back to crash within the French trenches. He succumbed to his wounds three days later.

As Noltenius indicated, Neuenhofen seems to have 'forced down' his opponent rather than shot him down. After the war Neuenhofen wrote an exaggerated account that probably refers to this day's fight. He claimed that he got behind one of the enemy fighters at 3000 metres and they entered into a *Kurvenkampf* (curving fight). Every time Neuenhofen managed to get into firing position, his opponent would spin down 300-400 metres, before pulling out and the dogfight would continue. According to Neuenhofen

Another view of the same *Jasta* 26 Fokker seen on page 51, taken during an enjoyable visit by some agreeable female medical personnel. The fighter was distinguished by a dark '5' marked just aft of the cockpit, which was repeated on the upper wing centre section in white. On 21 July, *Jasta* 26 lost one of its best performers when Otto Esswein was shot down in flames

this was repeated eight times until they were circling at treetop height. Then the enemy aircraft crashed into the trees without Neuenofen ever firing a shot.

21 July was far less successful for JG III. In the evening Ltn Harry von Bülow achieved the Wing's only success of the day when he killed Maj R H Freeman of No 73 Sqn – his Camel fell at Fère-en-Tardenois. The other members of Freeman's patrol reported that he was missing after a fight with several triplanes –

SPAD XIII No 8262 was flown by MdL André Conraux of *Escadrille* SPA83, who was forced down on 24 July by Hermann Frommherz. The *escadrille* emblem of a black griffin or dragon on a red circle on the fuselage bears evidence of some bullet hole patching. The insignia on the starboard side of the fuselage was souvenired for Frommherz' quarters

he was von Bülow's sixth, and final, victory. That did not, however, balance the loss of one of the topnotch aces of *Jasta* 26. Otto Esswein was killed at Hartennes, probably falling to Lt Henri Hay de Slade of SPA86 who claimed a Fokker in flames southeast of Belleu at 1745 hrs for his 11th victory. Esswein's talents would be sorely missed in the days to come.

The pleasant weather of 22 July allowed two aces to increase their personal scores. Vzfw Mesch of *Staffel* 26 brought his own tally to four with a SPAD at 0825 hrs and Carl Bolle attained his 22nd by wounding Camel pilot Lt W Kidder of No 73 Sqn, who was captured. On the 24th Noltenius glumly noted in his diary that, 'During the night our lines had to be withdrawn again. The whole Marne Front had to be abandoned'. Nonetheless, on that day Frommherz forced down MdL André Conraux of SPA83 behind German lines for his eighth success. Conraux's SPAD XIII 8262 landed intact and was taken to *Jasta* 'Boelcke's' airfield as a trophy.

'Once again the lines are withdrawn during the night – back to a line near Fère', wrote Noltenius on 25 July. In the air the JG III pilots struggled to hold back the enemy's incessant advance, Klimke shooting down an SE 5a from No 32 Sqn for his 11th kill at midday. In the evening Camel pilots from Nos 43 and 73 Sqns came out on the wrong end of a huge scrap with some of *Jasta* 'Boelcke's' experts, as well as *Jasta* 11. The official 'claim-book' of *Jasta* 'B' gives Carl Bolle credit for bringing down the Camel of 2Lt K S Laurie of No 73 Sqn, who was captured. Frommherz downed a No 43 Sqn Camel flown by Lt F S Coghill, who was captured. Gerhard Bassenge shot up another Camel, which burned after it crashed – this was probably D8197 from No 43 Sqn, 2Lt N Wilson being captured and later dying of his wounds. In addition, No 43 Sqn lost one more pilot and No 73 Sqn two, with all three airmen being killed.

Heavy rains gave the weary *Geschwader* pilots some much-needed time off for the next two days, but the aerial strife resumed on 28 July. Bolle and Frommherz picked up where they had left off, both of them downing SPADs that were counted as Bolle's 26th and Frommherz' tenth victories in the *Jasta* claim-book. In the squadron's own accounting system, Frommherz' victory was also registered as the 250th score by *Jasta* 'Boelcke'.

This rapid string of triumphs earned Hermann Frommherz new responsibilities – he was moved to *Jasta* 27 as its new permanent *Staffelführer* on 29 July. Four days later Noltenius noted, 'We moved our

At the beginning of August JG III occupied the airfield at Chambry, near Laon, where these *Jasta* 26 Fokkers were photographed. The machine in the centre bears a 'K' as a personal emblem. It is tempting to associate this D VII with Offz Stv Fritz Kublum, even though he had been transferred to a post with *Idflieg* on 6 July. Perhaps his former aircraft was still flown in its old markings?

airfield to Chambry, near Laon. For that reason we flew only once that morning and landed on the new field. The new field is large but not very good – the quarters are cramped but not bad'.

For the next seven days severely rainy weather limited aerial operations. On 3 August, however, Noltenius tried his hand at attacking a balloon. Although he saw his incendiaries disappear into the gasbag, it refused to burn due to the rains and the damp air. However, he perceptively noted, 'I had collected some experience which could be of value at a later date perhaps'.

THE BATTLE OF AMIENS

The restful period of inactivity came to an end in a big way on 8 August 1918. Ludendorff would famously call it the 'black day of the German Army – it put the decline of our fighting power beyond all doubt. The war must be ended'. The Battle of Amiens opened with a titanic artillery barrage at 0420 hrs British time. The assault was carried out by the British Fourth Army and the French First Army, with unprecedented use of tanks and aircraft. The RAF would play an immensely important role in this turning point, but it would pay a heavy price. The brunt of the attack was against the German 2nd Army, to the northwest of JG III's base in the 7th Army sector.

Noltenius' diary tells the tale of 8 August;

'In the afternoon at 1600 hrs, I joined an assembly of all *Staffel* leaders in the officers' mess. Only Frommherz was not there, being in Laon at the time. The enemy had achieved a breakthrough on the 2nd Army Front and we had received orders to move there immediately for support. No details were available – neither the new line nor whether we would be able to get there in time. With Loerzer on leave, Bolle gave orders that all of the *Geschwader* should fly to the Front as soon as possible. Under a low cloud ceiling we took off and flew in the direction of La Fère.'

The pilots utilised an advance landing field at Ercheu, where they refuelled their aircraft prior to taking off again. Towards evening they reached the battle area and headed into a 'witches' cauldron' of frenetic combats between massed formations. Klimke shot down an SE 5a from No 56 Sqn, while Fruhner attacked another from No 24 Sqn and 'wrapped it up' for his 14th victory. His fellow *Jasta* 26 ace Mesch claimed a 'Bristol' at 2015 hrs, while Vzfw Wilhelm Skworz from *Staffel* 36 tallied his first kill with another two-seater.

9 August saw even more intense action. 'We stood ready for takeoff at 0600 hrs', wrote Noltenius. 'Broken overcast at 2000 metres. We climbed over the clouds and flew toward the lines at quite some altitude. On arrival at the Front we dived through the clouds and, while being barely able to see the ground, we noticed an enemy section of four DH 9s directly in front of us. Then, as I looked about, an enemy machine came dead straight for me. I circled, and with that the two leading machines were too far off for an attack. While I was still circling, a DH 9 passed beneath me on my starboard side, with Frommherz in pursuit, and a foreign [unidentified] machine. I was almost as close, fired, and in my burst saw the opponent plunge down engulfed in flames. He virtually exploded. Then I lost the *Staffel*. I was halfway-believing that I had shot down the enemy, but when I expressed this belief I was called to account (reproved)'.

Staffelführer Frommherz believed that *he* was the victor over the DH 9, and did not take kindly to Noltenius counter-claiming it. In all, Noltenius flew five sorties that day and had several unsuccessful scraps with two-seaters. In regard to the triumphs of his own *Jasta* 27, he wrote, 'Score of the day – four enemy shot down. Frommherz, Klimke and Lux one two-seater each. Neuenhofen one Sopwith – 70th kill of the *Staffel*'. The DH 9s that fell to Frommherz, Klimke and Vzfw Albert Lux came from No 107 Sqn, a beleaguered unit that lost eight aircraft on this day as it was bombing the bridge at Brie. Klimke was also credited with an SE 5a several hours later, unmentioned by Noltenius.

Two more SE 5a fighters were credited to Mesch and Brandt of *Jasta* 26 at 1230 hrs. Carl Bolle and Otto Löffler were victorious over two-seaters, with Bolle claiming an 'RE' and Löffler describing his as an 'AW' (Armstrong-Whitworth FK 8).

Jasta 36 was in action as well, with Ltn Gutsche triumphing over the SPAD XIII of Brig H Pathais of SPA153, who was killed. However, Ltn d R Egon Patzer of *Jasta* 36 also died that day, having possibly become the third victim of Capt Battle, the CO of SPA103 of the famous *Cigognes* group.

Jasta 'Boelcke' fought not only the RAF but also ground forces on 9 August according to Bolle;

'English infantry, along with Americans, attacked the village of Rosières with ground attack aircraft and tanks. The tanks, covered by a range of hills, led against the village but were not observed by German artillery

Ltn Alfred Lindenberger had been posted to the 'Boelcke' *Staffel* in May 1918, and by 13 August he had succeeded in getting his friend Kurt Jentsch transferred to the unit. Jentsch had been Lindenberger's pilot when they both served in FA 234(A). D VII (OAW) 4453/18 was one of at least two Fokkers flown by Lindenberger. This photo was taken after the armistice when the D VII was in British hands – the guns have been removed and the cross on the rudder painted over. However, it still shows off the white nose of *Jasta* 'B' and the degraded striping on the fuselage, believed to be light yellow and black

and, thus, were not fired upon. After the ground attack aircraft retreated before our German *Staffel*, we dived as a unit onto the tanks and attacked them with machine guns. After the third attack the artillery, which had in the meantime obviously become aware of the tanks because of the continual dives made by our aircraft, laid down destructive fire in the area concerned. After a short time, three tanks were burning, two others remained motionless and the rest had turned around.'

After several frustrating disappointments, Noltenius finally attained his first officially recognised victory on 10 August. *Jasta* 27 was airborne at 0900 hrs, with Noltenius noting;

'I flew third left, because Schellenberg and Ritter were flying with us for the first time. Again, we flew over the clouds towards the front, and when there, dived through the clouds. An enemy squadron of six machines was in pursuit of four Fokkers rather deep into our side. We cut their retreat off. I dived as fast as I could towards them and was one of the first to get there. My plan was to get below the enemy aircraft and when there, to turn around, because I mistook them for two-seaters. I made a mistake, however, and circled too early.

'I throttled back, planning to let them pass overhead, but the Sopwith Dolphins planned differently. The second aeroplane immediately dived at me. By circling tightly I escaped him. His shots missed me and he dived away! I immediately put myself at his heels and off we went downward like crazy. I was able to maintain contact and to manoeuvre into position. The pilot turned his head, saw me, and at once put his aeroplane into a vertical dive. But I followed him, and close to the ground was once more in a firing position at very close range. I fired, passed him, flew a turn and saw him lying on his back hard north of Puzeaux near Chaulnes. The shot-down aeroplane was a Sopwith Dolphin with an "M" marking on the top wing (first confirmed victory!).

'Lux and Neuenhofen also shot one enemy aeroplane each. Thus the *Staffel* had, at this sector of the Front, scored nine victories, all on our side.'

The large Sopwith Dolphins (often mistaken for two-seaters) were from No 87 Sqn, which had two pilots captured on this date, not three. Still, Noltenius reported, 'Big party in the evening. It was Frommherz' anniversary and we had reason to celebrate the 70th kill of the *Staffel* [meanwhile the score was 73, though]. Very nice affair; good food, champagne, beer and music'. He also wrote that the first three days of the offensive had cost the RAF dearly, but that *Jasta* 27 was the most successful unit.

The celebrations on the 10th must have impressed the two recently arrived neophytes mentioned by Noltenius, Ltn d R Schellenberg and Vzfw Ernst de Ritter. Neither would become an ace, but Ritter would leave his impressions of life in JG III for modern historians. After the war he moved to the USA, where he anglicised his name to de Ridder. He lived in Richmond, Virginia, and was interviewed a few years before he died on 23 January 1968. A native of Düsseldorf, he had been fascinated by aviation at a young age, but was unable to enter the Air Service when war broke out. After almost three years serving in field artillery and flak units, Ritter finally obtained a transfer to the flying service and went to the *Fliegerschule* at Halberstadt in August 1917, then to the school at Hannover from October 1917 to January 1918. After a stint at the observers' school in Asch, he went to *AFP* 4 and then reported to Frommherz at *Jasta* 27.

According to Ritter, Frommherz was very respected by his men. He was strict about ensuring that his new pilots were ready before they made any frontline flights with the *Jasta*. Ritter was introduced to the D VII for the first time, and after three days of test flying he made his first patrol. Many years later, he recalled that the Fokkers of *Jasta* 27 had yellow engine cowlings and tails, and that his own had a white fuselage band with an eagle emblem on it, just aft of the cockpit. He also recalled that *Staffelführer* Frommherz had his top wing painted in alternating black and red vee stripes so that his men could identify him in the air.

On 11 August Noltenius reported that because of an expected offensive near Fismes, the *Geschwader* did not fly up to the 2nd Army front but patrolled between Rheims and Soissons. Erich Buder knocked down a Breguet at 1150 hrs for his sixth claim, while Oblt Bolle claimed a 'SPAD two-seater' near Fismes (possibly an American Salmson 2A2), confirmed as his 28th victory in the *Jasta* 'B' claims book. His 'RE' downed on 9 August was actually confirmed out of order as his 29th. With his 20th kill having been recorded back on 16 July, Bolle surely should have been under consideration for a *Pour le Mérite* by this time, but the award was still in his future.

The clear weather of 12 August brought forth few French aircraft on the 7th Army Front. In the evening at 1840 hrs *Jasta* 26 launched an attack on the French balloon line, and Riemer flamed the balloon of the 68e *Cie Aerostieres* for his third victory. Noltenius flew a solo sortie in search of his own balloon, only to find that the French had pulled them all down.

On the 13th, Noltenius recounted, 'In the morning, just before takeoff, we got the good tidings that we were to fly in front of the 2nd Army. We flew with *Jasta* 26 and *Jasta* "Boelcke", via St Quentin, Pèronne, along the Roman Road towards the Front. The whole sky was full of Fokkers. Small wonder that no Englishmen showed up'. The JG III pilots landed at the airfield of JG I at Bernes, where they learned that *Jasta* 11's Lothar von Richthofen had just been wounded by a bullet through his leg.

'At 1700 hrs we took off again and caught an SE 5 which Frommherz shot down. We flew a third sortie in the evening. Behind the lines we discovered an enemy long-range reconnaissance aeroplane, which flew overhead some 2000 metres higher up. Klimke, who was leading, pulled his aeroplane up really hard. The other aircraft were unable to stay with him. Klimke shot him down – the aeroplane exploded while diving to escape.'

Frommherz and *Jasta* 27 joined in in a running fight between *Jasta* 26 (led by Bruno Loerzer) and No 60 Sqn's SE 5a scouts. At 1720 hrs Loerzer shot down Lt E McCracken, who was lucky to survive as a PoW, while Fruhner probably attacked the SE 5a of Lt J R Anderson, which went down in flames near Chaulnes for his 15th victory. However, four days after his first victory, Ltn Gutsche of *Jasta* 36 had to parachute from his flaming aircraft during a combat – he landed safely, but his facial burns sent him to hospital.

A new aviator had arrived at *Jasta* 'Boelcke' on 13 August in the form of Vzfw Kurt Jentsch, who had already acquired extensive experience as a reconnaissance pilot and a *Jagdflieger* in *Jasta* 61. With some assistance from *Jasta* 'B's' Alfred Lindenberger (formerly his observer), Jentsch arranged a transfer to the prestigious *Staffel*. He later wrote;

'Soon I reach Chambry. I report to the leader of *Jagdstaffel* "Boelcke", Ltn Bolle. Afterwards, I have

The Battle of Amiens resulted in a target-rich environment for *Jasta* 'Boelcke's' Carl Bolle and the other JG III Fokker pilots. Bolle brought his score to 29 on 9 August – he is seen here with one of several D VIIs that bore his distinctive markings. The fuselage bands were black, white and yellow and the wings displayed formation leader's markings of two white stripes

to introduce myself to the *Geschwader Kommandeur*. The office is located nearby. I report to Oblt Dahlmann, the *Geschwader* adjutant, who has just come in, and he leads me to the *Geschwaderführer*.

'Oblt Loerzer, the commander of *Jagdgeschwader Nr* III, is sitting in a high-backed armchair at his desk. As I click my heels, he glances up. I report, according to regulations, "Pilot Vzfw Jentsch, from *Jagdstaffel* 61, transferred to *Jagdgeschwader* III". Oblt Loerzer acknowledges and welcomes me. The sun floods the room. Its rays mirror themselves in the *Pour le Mérite* that he is wearing. The charming and friendly manner with which I am received has immediately won me over to the commander. I have never before been greeted so affably and in such a relaxed manner by an officer in a superior position. After several questions concerning my training and previous positions held, I am dismissed.'

Jentsch took part in two sorties that very day.

On 14 August *Jastas* 26 and 27 again flew in support of the 2nd Army in the afternoon, and Noltenius laconically reported, '*Jasta* 26 had shot down seven (sic)'. Only four of those seven were confirmed. JG III commander Bruno Loerzer and Oblt Theodor Dahlmann, the *Geschwader* adjutant, both flew with *Jasta* 26 and each bested an SE 5a, as did Riemer (fourth victory). Erich Buder drove down a Breguet for his eighth. In addition, *Jasta* 27 neophyte Ernst de Ritter was brought down this day but returned unhurt to receive 'birthday greetings' – the traditional welcome for someone who had survived being shot down.

That same day, however, the pilots of *Jasta* 36 bade farewell to their esteemed and popular leader, Ltn d R Harry von Bülow. His last remaining brother Conrad, who had once commanded *Jasta* 19, had been killed in a flying accident in Finland. Because Harry was now the sole surviving brother, of four, he was taken out of harm's way by the high command. He would return to combat in World War 2, however, and score more victories in that conflict. He died on 27 February 1976.

The pilots of *Jasta* 36 had retained a few of their worn-out triplanes for some time. It is not known how many D VIIs they had at this date, but on 19 August Noltenius noted, '*Jasta* 36 gets Fokker parasols [E V] – we

A new and exciting type of aircraft arrived for the *Jasta* 36 pilots on 19 August 1918. This Fokker E V parasol fighter displays a personal marking of a dark star on a white band with dark borders. The cowling was probably painted in a somewhat lighter shade of the unit's traditional blue colour that produced a very light shade on contemporary film. After pilots in *Jastas* 6 and 19 were killed in E Vs that crashed due to wing failure, the new type was grounded pending a complete investigation

got 11 new engines for our D VIIs'. The pilots of *Staffel* 36 were excited by the look of these light, elegant monoplanes powered by Oberursel Ur III rotaries. *Jasta* 36 airmen who had the opportunity to fly the parasols considered them *blendend* (dazzling, or brilliant). However, such opportunities were short-lived.

On 16 August, Ltn Riedel of *Jasta* 19 perished when the wing of his E V structurally failed during a flight. On 19 August, Ltn Rolff of *Jasta* 6 died in another crash caused by wing failure. These events put the E V under a cloud of suspicion and the type was soon grounded. *Staffel* 36 had turned over some of its Dr Is in exchange for the E Vs, but it still had at least one Dr I and an E V on strength as late as mid-September. The extent of the parasols' use is not known, and it was probably extremely limited – evidence indicates that *Jasta* 36 flew at least some D VIIs in the next few weeks.

Examples of the new D VII equipped with the superb BMW IIIa engine had been arriving at JG III for some time. While the Mercedes-engined Fokkers were very potent machines, the BMW versions were game changers. The BMW IIIa delivered 185 hp at 1410 rpm and was designed so that power decrease with an increase in altitude was much reduced in comparison with other engines. Power did fall off somewhat at high altitude, but the engine still delivered 180 hp at 1800 metres. It is likely that *Jastas* 'Boelcke' and 26, at least, had full complements of BMW Fokkers, which accounts in part for their great success in late 1918. *Jasta* 27 probably had some as well, issued to formation leaders first.

Noltenius had long been planning tactics for attacking balloons, and on 20 August his efforts finally bore fruit for his second confirmed victory. He wrote;

'At 1130 hrs we got orders to take off because there seemed to be a hell of a lot of activity at the 9th Army [front]. The weather was cloudy, with mist starting at an altitude of 600 metres. [After he became separated from his *Staffel*] I decided to attack a balloon. I set my compass course near the

Friedrich Noltenius (at right, with walking stick) achieved his second confirmed victory on 20 August by flaming a French balloon. Here, he poses with his visiting brother in a photo possibly taken on 5 September. Noltenius' early OAW-built D VII was marked with his usual personal stripes, inspired by the flag of his birthplace of Bremen, in the Hanseatic League colours of red and white

ground, climbed over the cloud layer to 2000 metres and then started a glide to the point where the balloon ought to be (a most exciting flight, this). But when I broke clear of the clouds, I was still too short and had to apply full throttle once more and climb over the clouds. This time I came out quite close to the balloon, turned in its direction, aimed carefully and did not fire until I was at close quarters. I misjudged the distance, however.

'Suddenly, I realised that only a couple of metres separated us. I barely managed to pull up my machine and just missed the top of the balloon. I hastily climbed into the clouds and escaped without drawing flak fire. The balloon burned in only a small spot, which soon grew in size until a big flame soared up. The balloon stood at the northern edge of the forest of Villers-Cotterêts.'

That same day, Lindenberger of *Jasta* 'B' bested an AR 1 from *Escadrille* AR268 for his seventh victory, two days after he had downed a Breguet for his sixth.

THE BATTLE OF BAPAUME

The next British offensive would focus on the capture of Bapaume, and on 21 August a preliminary operation aimed at the Arras-Albert railway line began. On the German 7th Army Front, meanwhile, *Jasta* 27 attacked a formation of 15 Breguet bombers and Caudron escort aircraft, but with negligible results. Löffler of *Jasta* 'B' did, however, succeed in claiming a Breguet west of Champs for his fourth victory, and the next day Ernst Bormann of the same *Staffel* defeated a SPAD for his fourth too.

The British Third Army, supported by 100 tanks, began the Battle of Bapaume against the German 17th Army on 23 August. As part of the reinforcement of RAF units participating in the offensive, the USAS's 17th and 148th Aero Squadrons, which had been flying Sopwith Camels under British control, moved into the British Third Army area.

At noon on the 23rd the pilots of JG III were informed that they were to fly to Arras in response to the British attack, although that order was revoked in the afternoon. They would actually make the transfer to the 17th Army in stages over the next few days. Between the 23rd and the 25th all four *Staffeln* moved to new airfields in the area of Aniche/Emerchicourt, ten kilometres southeast of Douai. Noltenius reported that *Jasta* 27 flew to Aniche on 24 August and rested the next day. According to Kurt Jentsch, *Jasta* 'Boelcke' flew to the new field at Emerchicourt on the 25th. 'The airfield is broad and lies favourably', he wrote. 'One can take off and land from all corners of the sky. In the southern part of Aniche – a small town and the intersection of several railway lines – we take up our pilots' quarters.'

The next day – 26 August – the entire *Geschwader* flew its first sortie in the new sector and clashed with elements of the 148th and 17th Aero Squadrons. This day would always be remembered by the British-trained Americans as a disaster for the 17th in particular. The 148th's pilots had been ordered to carry out low-level strafing attacks east of Bapaume, and a flight of four Camels had arrived in the area at mid-afternoon just as elements of JG III reached the same spot. Assisted by a strong westerly wind, the Fokkers of *Jasta* 27 swooped down on the Camels and a furious scrap began.

'Frommherz dived and shot down a Sopwith', reported Noltenius. Frommherz' target was 2Lt George V Seibold, a promising three-victory pilot who became the 148th's first fatality. Now, however, a flight of nine Camels from the 17th Aero Squadron arrived on the scene at an altitude of 1800 metres, just in time to witness Seibold's last desperate struggles against five Fokkers far below. The 17th's Camels had taken off to assist and protect the 148th's trench-strafers, being led by 1Lt W Tipton, with 2Lt Robert M Todd as deputy flight leader. Those in the rear of the formation sighted the rest of JG III heading toward them from Queant, and fired bursts in an attempt to warn Tipton. However, the latter was intent on saving Seibold and led them down in a steep dive.

'Bob' Todd, a five-victory ace, would write many years later;

'When we reached the lines at Bapaume, we saw five Huns attacking [Seibold]. Just as we reached them, 30 or 40 Huns came down on us from out of the clouds. They were a mixture of several groups, the checkerboards, the yellow noses etc. – all Fokker D VII biplanes. They were equal to anything we could do, so when we turned into them I knew we were in for a big fight. I lost Tipton almost immediately, and started firing steadily for there were Huns everywhere I flew. I dove on one Hun who was on the tail of a Camel and got him out of control. He went over on his back and then went down nose first out of sight. I continued to fire and take evasive action – we could turn sharper than the Fokkers but they could out climb and out dive us.

'Someone finally got me as my motor quit and down I went. While I was at about 500 ft elevation, heading west, two Huns followed me down and started taking turns shooting at me. I took as many evasive turns as my motor would stand to keep them from lining up on me. They turned back when we reached the lines but the ground troops continued to fire at me. Finally my motor quit and down I had to go. There was no place to land so I held the aeroplane up off the ground as long as I could but my landing gear hit some barbed wire and over onto my back I went. I was left hanging upside down above a trench.'

Todd was taken prisoner by German troops who yanked him out of his aeroplane, breaking his foot in the process – his Camel may have been one of three credited to Frommherz.

Noltenius presented his own perspective of the events just after Frommherz shot down Seibold;

'We had barely assembled again when strong enemy single-seater units dropped on us. Frommherz and Klimke rushed at them with perfect timing, while I missed the proper moment. Terrific dogfighting followed, in the course of which Frommherz downed two opponents. Klimke and I followed another one [possibly 2Lt H P Bittinger, who was killed in action].

One of the participants in JG III's decimation of the 17th Aero Squadron on 26 August was Ltn Rudolf Klimke, who was credited with his 16th kill. Here, Klimke poses in front of his yellow-nosed *Jasta* 27 Fokker. Although the photo is regrettably indistinct, it appears that Klimke's usual anchor emblem was carried in black on a yellow band aft of the cockpit and that the tail was probably a very pale yellow. The striking chevron markings on the top wing were probably the insignia of a *Kette* leader (*courtesy B Schmäling*)

He manoeuvred so smartly that it was nearly impossible to close in. Occasionally, he would rush one of us and fire. Finally, when he flew straight for a moment to run for home, Klimke and I got behind him and he plunged down burning.'

In addition, 2Lt H H Jackson was killed when his Camel F1958 was shot down by Ltn d R Fritz Heinz of *Jasta* 'Boelcke'. Tipton was wounded in both legs and taken prisoner, being reunited with Todd in captivity. 1Lt H B Frost, who suffered terrible wounds, was taken prisoner and eventually died on 2 October. 1Lt L C Roberts was killed. Frommherz was credited with three Camels while Bruno Loerzer, Klimke, Heinz and Bolle claimed one each. This was the worst single day in the war for any American fighter squadron. Kurt Jentsch wrote, 'With these victories, *Jagdstaffel* "Boelcke" has achieved more than 260 aerial victories since it has come into existence'.

For JG III, the fighting on this new front had started with seven victories without a loss. Even this was bettered on 27 August with eight victims credited. Once again, Camel units suffered the attention of the *Geschwader* pilots. *Jasta* 26 experts Lange and Riemer defeated Sopwiths (probably from No 208 Sqn), while Classen and Fruhner claimed SE 5as. Classen's SE 5a was also claimed by Noltenius, but once again he was denied credit. *Jasta* 36 was back in the scoring column with two Camels (possibly from Nos 54 and 73 Sqns) credited to Quandt and one more to Flgr Ludwig Möhring. For Frommherz' 16th victory, he forced down Bristol F 2B Fighter E2514 'K' from No 22 Sqn, the aircraft's fuselage being displayed on the *Staffel* airfield. The Bristol's pilot, Lt F M Sellars, was captured, but his observer, 2Lt T Collis, was killed.

There was good cause for celebration in *Jasta* 'Boelcke' on the 28th, when Ltn Carl Bolle was awarded the *Pour le Mérite* (with his score at 31). In the evening the *Staffel* hosted an elegant party attended by the staff of JG III, Göring and other notables from nearby units. The war was put on hold for a few carefree hours.

Bristol F 2B Fighter E2514 from No 22 Sqn was shot down by Hermann Frommherz – now in command of *Jasta* 27 – near Graincourt at 0705 hrs on 27 August 1918. Its battered fuselage was brought to the JG III airfield, while its pilot, Lt F M Sellars, was taken prisoner and the observer, 2Lt T B Collis, was killed

On 29 August Noltenius recorded yet another victory dispute, and its resolution. 'First takeoff at 1000 hrs. Lux shot down a Bristol Fighter – he rolled dice with Stoltenhoff to see who would get the kill. Lux won the toss, and the victim'. This was victory number four for Lux. On the same day, Oblt Loerzer added two Sopwiths to bring his total to 33, while his adjutant, Theo Dahlmann, got another one for his third.

During the evening of 30 August there was a dense ground haze, but *Jasta* 27 was out looking for trouble. Noltenius wrote;

'We made our approach at high altitude, then, because nothing could be seen from there, we dived. I lost the *Staffel.* I was on the verge of turning back when flak fire told me a Bristol Fighter was there. He was dropping leaflets. At an altitude of 1000 metres, I caught him head on, and by a turn placed myself below him, and then I slowly gained altitude, all the time carefully following his turns. Soon I got a chance to fire. The Bristol then spun and recovered, perhaps intentionally, in order to get me in an overhead position. I dived below him. The observer stuck his hands up as a sign of surrender, but as the aeroplane continued to fly toward enemy territory, I had to resume my fire. I closed in to an aeroplane's length, fired, and the Bristol Fighter spun down without recovering. It dropped into the cratered terrain south of Etaing, north of the Arras-Cambrai Road (third confirmed victory).'

In spite of Noltenius' description, it seems this was a DH 4 from No 57 Sqn – pilot Lt Devitt was wounded while observer Sgt Lovesey was injured as they crashed within their own lines. At the very same time as this combat, a No 64 Sqn SE 5a was falling to the unerring aim of Otto Fruhner of *Jasta* 26 for his 18th victory.

No 64 Sqn lost another SE 5a the next day, but this one was bested by Noltenius – whose luck was improving. He reported;

'First takeoff at 1500 hrs. Very cloudy. We flew as a group of five. Apparently an SE 5a had seen us. The *Staffel* set course on it. I saw Frommherz attack him and thought that the Englishman would climb over the clouds. So I immediately took course toward enemy territory and climbed over the clouds. It did not take long, and he did appear there. I attacked him and pursued him downward. He went down in a terrific dive. I gained on him, fired and that apparently got him so confused that he rammed into the ground. This happened deep in enemy territory, and I was in a hurry to get out of there (fourth confirmed victory).'

Capt T Bunbury was killed in the fiery crash. *Jasta* 'B's' Lindenberger was also successful, downing an RE 8.

Kurt Jentsch wrote of these days;

'By the end of August, the Englishmen have already taken up positions in front of the new German defensive line at Bapaume-Combles-Maurepas. But the battle is still not over. Every day brings new fights. After drumfire from artillery, the Tommies overrun our front with their tanks and new divisions. Who the devil knows where they all come from?'

In the air, ironically, the pilots of JG III were in top form, and reaching peak efficiency. In the last six days of August, 23 enemy aircraft were credited to the *Geschwader*, although their strenuous efforts were unable to influence events on the ground. Even so, their greatest days were ahead of them.

CHAPTER FOUR

SEPTEMBER SUCCESS STORY

On 1 September Vzfw Skworz and Ltn Quandt of *Jasta* 36 both recorded victories. It is believed that this rare view shows two *Jasta* 36 D VIIs. Both machines were marked with blue noses, as well as a broad fuselage band which may also have been blue. The D VII in the foreground was Fokker-built, while the OAW-built machine in the distance was marked with a flamboyant chequerboard pattern on its tail surfaces

September 1918 would be the most successful month of the war for JG III. It was not alone among German fighter units in this, for September was the worst month for casualties in the Allied air services during World War 1 – yet at its end only six more weeks of fighting remained.

During the afternoon of 1 September, at about 1345 hrs, Bristol F 2B Fighters of No 62 Sqn were escorting DH 4s of No 57 Sqn on a bomb run to Cambrai when they were enaged by elements of *Jastas* 'Boelcke', 26 and 36. *Geschwader* commander Bruno Loerzer led the interception, and he bested one of the Bristols for his 35th success – his opponents may have been pilot Lt L W Hudson and gunner 2Lt J Hall, who was wounded prior to their F 2B crashing behind British lines. At the same time *Jasta* 'B's' Ernst Bormann made 'ace' by downing another Bristol behind the German lines south of Lecluse, wounding the gunner, 2Lt D S Hamilton, who was captured, along with pilot 2Lt L B Raymond.

One of the No 57 Sqn bombers fell to Vzfw Skworz from *Jasta* 36, the DH 4 coming down at Brunémont, where the crew of 2Lts J Dugdale and F Robinson were taken prisoner. About two hours later *Jasta* 36 scrapped with No 32 Sqn, Ltn Quandt forcing down SE 5a E5939 of 2Lt John O Donaldson – a USAS pilot with seven victories. He was taken prisoner. Another American ace in No 32 Sqn, Lt Bogart Rogers, was part of this fight, and he wrote that they were attacked by 'Seven Fokker biplanes, very good machines and very good pilots.'

2 September was a day of particular significance for the military forces of Imperial Germany, especially the Prussians. On 1 September 1870, during the Franco-Prussian War, the forces of King Wilhelm of Prussia had defeated the army of emperor Napoleon III at Sedan in a pivotal battle. In 1871, the recently-united Germans of the Empire could not quite agree on a common *German* holiday, but the victory at Sedan would be commemorated as a memorial holiday, designated *Sedantag*, on 2 September every year. It duly became something of a de facto national holiday. By a happy coincidence, the airmen of JG III would compile their greatest single-day total on Sedan Day 1918.

At 0600 hrs (German time) on 2 September, the Canadian Corps of the British 1st Army and the 18th Corps of the 3rd Army attacked the Drocourt-Quéant Line – an immensely well-fortified set of mutually defensive lines abreast of the Cambrai-Arras road. The British Army fired 934,857 shells this day, and the Canadians were strongly supported by tanks and aircraft.

JG III airmen would fly three main missions on the 2nd and chalk up an amazing 26 victories out of the 35 or so German claims made against the British. In studying the multitude of German claims and Allied losses on such a day – beset with clouds and rain, and full of frenzied and confused fighting – it is impossible to reconcile them with infallible accuracy. An overview is presented here, therefore, with comments from those who were there when possible. Any times quoted are from German time, which was one hour ahead of Allied time during this period.

Although the weather was very poor, the first combat recorded by a JG III pilot was timed at 0820 hrs by Theodor Quandt. He may have been part of a squadron patrol from *Jasta* 36 that was out early in the day, as the major sorties in *Geschwader* strength took place later. Quandt claimed a Camel (probably from No 209 Sqn) at Ecourt St Quentin. The squadron lost two Camels shot down in flames at exactly that location at about the same time. On this same sortie, due to the thick clouds and mist, Quandt also mistakenly engaged a German Rumpler two-seater from *FA(A)* 210. Despite the *Jasta* 36 ace breaking off his attack as soon as he realised his error, he had wounded the observer. The pilot landed the Rumpler safely, however. His attack on the German aircraft immediately brought Quandt under fire from another D VII, but he escaped into the cloud cover.

Regarding the later sorties carried out *en masse*, Bruno Loerzer wrote;

'On Sedan Day, 1918, we made three big sorties – in the forenoon between 0900 and 1000 hrs, again between 1100 and 1300 hrs and then between 1700 and 1900 hrs. The weather was poor, with clouds down to 500 metres. Rain prevented [getting] a good view. The *Geschwader* flew in close formation of 30 aeroplanes to the battlefield. While at an altitude of about 500 or 600 metres, we sighted an enemy formation of about 20 machines in loose array. We took care to await the opportunity of attacking them with the advantage of surprise on our side. Seconds later I gave the

Oblt Bruno Loerzer and the men of *Jagdgeschwader Nr* III had their best day on 2 September 1918. On that 'Sedan Day' the *Geschwader* was credited with 26 confirmed victories. Historian Lance Bronnenkant has determined that this photo was likely taken in Berlin sometime between 10-13 July, when Loerzer was attending the Adlershof fighter trials (*L Bronnenkant*)

signal to attack, and we immediately immersed in a wild, whirling dogfight. More than 50 aircraft were twisting, diving and turning madly in the sky. Wind squalls made the task difficult and heightened the constant danger of a mid-air collision. In a fight of this type, discipline, cooperation and cool self-control are the deciding factors. Our better discipline and cooperation on this occasion netted us 12 enemy machines in this first fight of the day.'

Jasta 26 pilots were in battle first against SE 5as from No 40 Sqn, which lost Lt H W Clark (he died of his wounds). *Staffel* 26 aces Lange and Fruhner were both credited with kills (at 1015 hrs and 1025 hrs, respectively) at Villers. *Jasta* 27 pilots were also active in this scrap with the RAF formations, which apparently included Bristols from No 22 Sqn. Noltenius wrote;

'We took off before it had barely stopped raining. At the Front, when we first peeked out of the clouds, we saw two Bristol Fighters. Frommherz dived on one of them and shot it down. Once I was below him in a good position for firing. It would have been better to have attacked the five SE 5s that flew at our port side. Frommherz then returned [to the airfield], as he had emptied his guns.

'I remained at the Front. English single-seaters soon arrived in large numbers. I then saw two German *Staffeln* arrive, *Jasta* "Boelcke" and *Jasta* 36. I immediately flew over to them, as their arrival promised aerial battles. It did not take long, *Jasta* 36 starting a dive toward two Sopwiths. I dived also and attained such a speed that I was there before the *Staffel* arrived. I hit one of the aeroplanes, which began smoking, but turned off at once because I knew darn well how many were still up there in the clouds. A sergeant of *Jasta* 36 saw him burn [this was Noltenius' fifth confirmation].

'I then climbed to just below the clouds and flew southward. After a while I observed a DH 4 that crossed the lines toward our territory. I immediately detoured towards the Front and cut him off. By a shallow dive I gained momentum and positioned myself behind him in a turn. Löffler attacked simultaneously with me. By firing his guns he prevented me from diving, for I would have flown into the path of his bullets. But I kept contact with the enemy and finally forced myself into position, this being my privilege [as the first attacker]. I forced him down until he somersaulted in a crash-landing.'

The distinctive D VIIs of *Jasta* 26 and their pilots played an important part in the achievements of 2 September. Including Bruno Loerzer and his adjutant Theodor Dahlmann (who flew with *Jasta* 26), the pilots of this *Staffel* were credited with ten victories. This photo reveals two *Jasta* 26 D VIIs in post-war British hands, probably at Nivelles, where many JG III aircraft were turned over after the armistice. The aircraft with the zigzag marking at right had its serial number re-marked on the fin – it may be D VII (F) 4254/18, a BMW-engined machine

Having dissuaded Ltn d R Otto Löffler from horning in on his fight, Noltenius was credited with this two-seater downed at Rumaucourt at 1120 hrs.

As for the second major sortie of the day, Loerzer wrote;

'During the afternoon flight, however, we found the element of surprise had switched to the enemy, who suddenly dived down on us in a well-closed formation. It was now imperative that we remained together. We flew as close as we dared, and set up a shield of machine gun fire against them. Their formation wavered and was overtaken by a moment of indecision. We turned and pushed into their ranks, and in the ensuing fight the enemy lost a further 14 machines shot down.'

It seems these 14 claims were all made in a hectic 30 minutes between 1220 hrs and 1250 hrs. As usual, Oblt Loerzer and his adjutant Oblt Dahlmann were flying with *Jasta* 26 – this *Staffel* was credited with six Camels in five minutes. At 1240 hrs Dahlmann's Sopwith fell at Haucourt, at the very same time and place as Vzfw Mesch's first Camel victory of the day. Two minutes later Mesch defeated another Sopwith at Haucourt, and at 1245 hrs Oblt Loerzer and Ltn d R Ehlers sent Camels down northeast of Barelle. *Jasta* 'Boelcke's' Löffler downed three Camels this day to bring his total to seven. His fellow *Jasta* 'B' ace Ernst Bormann also claimed three more Camels to raise his tally to eight.

As for their opponents, for the second time in eight days, a Camel unit of British-trained Americans had suffered a beating at the hands of JG III, but this time it was the turn of the 148th Aero Squadron. Two flights from the unit were returning from bombing and strafing the retreating enemy on the Albert-Cambrai road when they were bounced. 'A' Flight, led by 1Lt Field Kindley (12 victories), had just reached the shelter of a large cloud bank south of Rumaucourt, but 'B' Flight, led by the famous ace 1Lt Elliott White Springs (16 victories), was trailing below. At 1245 hrs Springs sighted four Fokkers dropping out of the clouds – he led his flight against them, but then sighted several more groups diving down, for what he claimed was a total of 25 D VIIs. All evidence indicates these were from *Jastas* 26 and 'Boelcke'. Kindley spotted 'B' Flight's predicament and banked his Camel sharply to the right, his flight plummeting down into the melee.

In his flight log, Springs laconically, but aptly, reported, '1 hr 35 min. Canal du Nord. Disaster itself. Forster, Kenyon, Frobisher, Mandel missing'. He was more descriptive in a letter to his father;

'The wind and numbers were against us but the Huns were after our low machines, so I had to take them on. Plainly the Huns meant business and so did we. As soon as I would get on the tail of one Hun, another would get me, and as soon as I would shake him off there would be another. Forster shot one down off my tail and then got in a bad position himself. He dove under me and I took the one on his tail. But before I could get him there was one on my tail, shooting at 25 yards range. I could see the tracers going two feet over my head. I had to circle twice under him before he stopped firing and pulled up. I looked at my wings, and my left lower wing had buckled, but

Theodor Hermann Dahlmann served as the adjutant for JG III until the end of the war. He shot down a Camel at 1240 hrs at Haucourt for his contribution to the 'Sedan Day' triumphs. He is known to have flown a BMW D VII in *Jasta* 26 colours, marked with a Norse Valkyrie helmet in black with the legend *Walküre* beneath it

my aeroplane held together. I'm the only one of my Flight who returned. "A" Flight lost one man and claims three Huns.'

Out of Springs' flight, 2Lt J D Kenyon was a wounded prisoner, 2Lt O Mandel was also a PoW, 1Lt L H Forster had been killed and 2Lt J Frobisher would later die of his wounds. These losses match both some of the *Jasta* 26 claims and Bormann's untimed victories. The one loss from 'A' Flight was 1Lt Jesse O Creech (seven victories, and possibly Löffler's opponent), who actually survived his crash in British lines. Creech later reported;

'I undertook to dive out of the mass of swirling aeroplanes and climb to the top, but two Germans spied this manoeuvre and drove me back into the middle of the flight. Shortly after this I fell on the tail of a Fokker and just as I got my sights adjusted and let go a burst, all the instruments in front of my face began to disappear. I quickly kicked my right-hand rudder in, and when I turned my head I found that two enemy fliers were sitting on my tail, pumping lead into my dashboard. The bullets, which had riddled my instrument panel completely, wrecked my oil tank, and the engine of my Camel soon overheated and stopped. At 17,000 ft in the air, I had a problem on my hands to escape and glide into Allied territory. I was able to cross the Canal du Nord at a height of about 100 ft, finally crashing into shell holes towards the back of the line.'

1Lt Kindley returned to his airfield and claimed one Fokker, but he wrote, 'I found 36 holes in my bus. Ten had burst on the butt of my guns and the splinters sprinkled my face, while one bullet went through my goggles, missing my temple by a quarter-of-an-inch. My machine could not be flown again'. Three D VIIs were claimed by 'A' Flight pilots, but JG III had no reported casualties. The *Jasta* 'B' and *Jasta* 26 pilots also over-claimed in this fight, with ten victories for five Camels actually downed (plus Kindley's aircraft badly shot up). Nonetheless, all ten claims were confirmed by *Kogenluft* and contributed to the day's total.

Jasta 27 had also been busy. No 52 Sqn had sent out nine RE 8s to bomb Vitry, but the last group of three was savaged by *Staffel* 27. All three were shot down in their own lines – one crew crashed unhurt, another had a wounded observer and in the third, both crewmen were wounded. Stoltenhoff received credit for one RE 8 (second victory), while Lux was recorded as downing one RE and one 'Bristol' to raise his total to six. In addition, *Jasta* 58's Ltn Martin Demisch also seems to have claimed one of the RE 8s.

The Fokker pilots returned home, no doubt exhausted but jubilant. Their D VIIs were refuelled and rearmed as the pilots refreshed themselves and readied for the third sortie of the day. Oblt Loerzer described it;

'On our third flight of the day, we found ourselves alone in the heavens. So we used our freshly replenished guns against available ground targets. We dived onto advancing reserves, on marching columns and many other formations. From an altitude of 20 metres we fired on enemy tanks, bringing about considerable confusion in the rear area of the enemy, and giving relief to our own troops.'

Ltn d R Rudolf Stoltenhoff of *Jasta* 27 claimed his second confirmed victim on 2 September when he downed an RE 8. He had been acting commander of *Jasta* 27 from 6 July to 27 July 1918 and ended the war with three victories. Stoltenhoff is pictured here with his Dr I of *Jasta* 27 at Halluin-Ost in May 1918 (*B Schmäling*)

The impressive accomplishments of 2 September were reported in the following day's *Heeresbericht* (Army Report), and congratulatory telegrams were received from the Crown Prince as well as from the Chief of the General Staff, Field Marshall Paul von Hindenburg, whose message read as follows;

'May I express my full appreciation to JG III for the outstanding performance of 2 September, as shown by the loss to the enemy of 26 aircraft without any loss to ourselves. The behaviour of the commander, Oberleutnant B Loerzer, who, finding no aerial activity over the battle area, joined the battle against enemy tanks and ground forces, remains an example to all *Geschwader* commanders.'

Modern historians may critique the veracity of some of the claims, but the fact remains that under the contemporary standards of *Kogenluft*, the airmen of *Jagdgeschwader Nr* III were credited with an unparalleled 26 victories in one day. It was a record unmatched by either JGs I or II throughout the war.

No doubt the events of 2 September 1918 took on something of a legendary status within the *Geschwader*, the topic of many exaggerated retellings in the officers' *Kasino*. One *Jasta* 36 pilot who heard these tales was Vzfw Hans Brzenk. Although he only served with *Staffel* 36 from 11 October to 21 October 1918, when the unit was equipped with the Pfalz D XII, Brzenk also flew in other *Staffeln* from March 1918 until war's end. Well acquainted with the culture of the *Jagdflieger*, he flew in Germany's border conflict with Poland after the armistice.

In 1925 Brzenk wrote a memoir entitled *Im Kampf wider Kokarde und weisse Adler*. Like many similar works, it is an anecdotal account, short on specific dates and details. One of the chapters is entitled 'A Day of Great Battle: Aviator's Sedan Celebration 1918'. It provides an impressionistic tale of the fighting on 2 September, based not on his own experiences but on accounts he heard from others. Brzenk was not interested in presenting a blow-by-blow historical record, but rather an evocative story, incorporating what he knew of *Geschwader* operations from his own experiences in the unit. In order to flesh out the dry details of victories and losses, and to

Jasta 36 pilot Hans Brzenk recalled that the Fokkers of *Jasta* 26 bore black/white stripes 'like a Prussian sentry box', and *Geschwaderführer* Loerzer's D VII also had stripes on the wings. This D VII, photographed at Nivelles after the war, was almost certainly one of several flown by Loerzer, as evidenced by the stripes just visible on the underside of the lower wing (*courtesy of the 1914-1918 Aviation Heritage Trust*)

provide a window into *Geschwader* operations, portions of Brzenk's vivid and atmospheric account are presented here – translated by Adam Wait – with the *caveat* that it should be appreciated primarily as a flyer's tale;

'On the broad airfield the pilots are standing around and looking towards the west. There – suddenly an invisible hand dabs little cotton balls on the blue sky, so swiftly and hastily that the eye can hardly keep up. Little clouds of shrapnel and shell bursts! Anti-aircraft guns sent them puffing there, and now the gentle morning wind brings over the light cracking sound. Its short, sharp tone provides a distinct contrast to the rumbling of the larger guns.

'Strained glances pierce the air above. Nothing can yet be seen of the enemy. Binoculars are brought over. "An English formation." "Two-seaters, six . . . seven . . . eight machines!" "Ten Sopwiths from the right!" "Twelve single-seaters straight ahead!"

'The voices buzz excitedly all around. Mechanics hurry on by with the scarves, goggles, fur boots and gloves. Commands ring out. The field telephone bleats – "Are the other *Staffeln* ready? What is their fighting strength? Is everyone ready for takeoff?"

'The commander waves. The pilots are already swinging into their seats. The mechanics busily fasten the seat belt and attach the parachute, which serves as a seat cushion for the pilot. A short engine test suffices. The mechanics enjoy the confidence of the pilots. After a long period of fighting one has grown close to them.

'Some pilots are already waiting impatiently for the first one to take off, because the take off must exactly follow the prescribed sequence. There is a wave – "Well, take off already!" The first machine thunders away at full revs and lifts off after a short run. The others follow close behind, often rocking in the slipstream of the man in front. The noise is deafening. As they wait, they circle the airfield like hungry vultures. They all have to wait for the commander, Oblt Loerzer, who is the last one to take off. Like all of the other machines of his old *Staffel* 26, his aircraft is also striped black and white on the fuselage like a Prussian sentry box. To distinguish it from the others, the commander's machine also has stripes on the wings. And so the commander finally lifts into the air as the last one.

'A signal flare is fired from the earth, and like birds of prey the others dive down to take up position behind their leader. They must continuously maintain the right distance and exercise good formation discipline in every turn. Now the spectator on the ground sees the formation high in the air like a swarm of migratory birds in the form of a wedge. Every adjustment of the throttle forwards or backwards by the leader is faithfully imitated by every pilot.

'Little light clouds drift over from the west at 1200 metres height. Beneath them many gusts still pelt the formation, but in the instant they have climbed above them, the air is quite still and calm, and the pilot sits in his machine as though in an auto with perfect suspension on a smooth asphalt road. The small, light Fokker D VII easily obeys the slightest pressure on the controls.

'The horizon stretches beyond measure. One can hear nothing of the artillery fire. Just the even roar of the engine fills the pilot's ears through his head covering. The flight pays close attention to its leader. He flies obliquely along the front – i.e., that undefined, half-felt, half-estimated aerial zone above the lines in which only a sharp eye, lightning quick assessment of the situation and cool daring can help the flyer accomplish his tasks.

'A look around! There are English formations in dense swarms, an astonishing number of aerial forces. Like throngs of little points, from whose barely perceptible silhouette a practiced eye can soon recognise the type, they sit on the horizon, partially higher, partially lower. Some formations seem to heave to with a desire to attack. The commander maintains his course unwaveringly. Somewhere, his sharp, calculating eye must detect favourable opportunities. Halfway to the right behind the black-and-white *Staffel* there is a fairly dense band of Fokkers with white noses – *Jagdstaffel* "Boelcke".

'Suddenly, the commander's machine rocks steadily to the left and right a few times. Pay attention! That's the attack signal! Good God, where is there an enemy that close? Right, a formation of Sopwiths is coming up from below. On the wings painted brown on top, the red, white, and blue cockades are already flashing quite close. One of them pulls his machine up like a fish gulping some air and opens fire. But only a few threads of smoke, left behind by incendiary ammunition, lie in the empty air. Spirited fellows, these Englishmen!

'The lead German machine drops its nose, suddenly rushes down, and in an instant sits behind an Englishman and "wraps him up". Now pay attention. The whole band dives down after him in a whirl. Already there are blue and white stripes of smoke in the air from the tracer ammunition, a distinguishing mark of a scene of aerial combat. One's breath grows hot and pulses race. Gunsights search for an opponent. Now it is a matter of paying attention amidst the turmoil so that one can get a hold of and hang on to one's opponent, without being surprised from behind or colliding with the others.

'There is a Sopwith. Now get in close for a good shot! Come up behind him at full revs – the cockades loom large in the sights of the diving machine. But the enemy is alert. He already lies in a turn. The pursuer follows him mechanically. There, another Sopwith, who, in an opposing turn, is approaching perilously close. Will there be a collision? The Tommy is probably not aware of the danger. Now use the elevators, pull the stick into your body so that the turn will be as tight as possible. But the danger of a collision grows. The enemy goes into a turn, and he too is pressed up so firmly against the air that he cannot get away by any other means. The bright cockades on his lower wings grow menacingly, and the pairs of wheels of the undercarriages almost touch one another. One's breath

The BMW-engined D VIIs of *Jasta* 26 proved very potent weapons on 'Sedan Day'. Here is another BMW Fokker bearing the markings of *Staffel* 26, photographed as part of the interned collection of JG III aircraft at Nivelles after the armistice. The fin and rudder were outlined in black and an attempt has been made to obliterate the crosses

falters for an instant, but then the greatest danger has passed, and the two machines part again at racing speed.

'There are countless machines all around, both German and English. Suddenly, there is a Sopwith in the middle of the field of fire. Now keep calm and approach him. An iron will prevents one's finger from pressing the trigger. Firing at this point would still be a waste of ammunition. But now the enemy cockades have grown considerably. The opponent is on his guard. Like a frightened moth he flutters to the right and left. He does his turns and rolls. The pursuer mechanically follows all his moves until he is right on target.

'The machine guns rattle away and the joy of combat flashes through one's pounding heart. One's eye peers through the streams of smoke streaking backwards. Hasn't he yet begun to "stink" [pilots' jargon for burn], isn't he falling apart? In the meantime, a lightning quick glance in all directions to see whether danger threatens from some quarter. Get in closer. Perhaps [one] opened fire too soon after all! Now the cockades are gigantic. Every movement of the pilot can be seen. The hammering machine gun burst feels its way along the fuselage. There . . . one cockade remains behind and detaches from the fuselage along with the wing. There is a jerk and the machine inclines heavily forward with a single wing to begin a furious whirling descent into the depths – victory!

'And now immediately upwards in a curve with a glance down below. "Where is the impact?" That is important for confirmation of the victory. Suddenly, there is a sharp, hard cracking. Streaks of smoke whiz through the left wings, the fabric rips open in long holes and a round enters the steel tube fuselage close by the pilot's seat with a dull crack that is also felt by the hand on the controls. Damn it, not paying attention. A lightning quick reflex movement and the machine is immediately rolled to the right out of the dangerous burst. While turning, one's eye seeks out the opponent, but he cannot be seen amidst the whirling dance.

JG III's BMW-engined D VIIs certainly proved their worth on 2 September. This study of BMW-engined Fokker D VII (F) 4348/18 of *Jasta* 'Boelcke' shows off its white nose and Heine airscrew – it was taken at the end of the war, not long before it would be turned over to British forces after the armistice. The pilot's marking was the coat-of-arms of Berlin, a black bear on a crowned shield. Although the unidentified pilot is not pictured with the groundcrew, it is very likely he was Oblt Kurt von Griesheim, a native Berliner

Jasta 'Boelcke' pilots claimed seven victories on 'Sedan Day'. Here is beautiful BMW-engined Jasta 'B' D VII (F) 4361/18, whose unknown pilot chose a poor landing spot. The personal markings of red and white stripes were extended to the interplane struts and wheel covers, while the centre section struts were white. As with other BMW D VIIs of the Jasta, the serial number was re-marked in small characters on top of the rudder (courtesy of J Leckscheid)

'High above, the others rage with their opponents. Some English "aces" are among them, recognisable as leaders by the streamers on their wings. Several black trails of smoke stand in the sky, a sign that aircraft are going down in flames here. There . . . yet another. Stricken by a hit in the fuel tank, the aeroplane flares up brightly, has disappeared in a black cloud and the pieces whirl around in a confused jumble. The fuselage shoots down glowing like a meteor, leaving a long black cloud along its path.

'Other formations join in. Jasta "Boelcke" is sitting among them and is cleaning up. Everywhere there are machines turning and fighting and spinning, burning, and disintegrating opponents. A look reveals with satisfaction that no crashing Fokkers are yet to be seen.

'Finally, only German machines are to be found in the hustle and bustle above the Arras–Cambrai road. Whatever Englishmen were not rescued by a swift dive westwards lie smashed on the ground. The battle brought everyone far below. One is astonished to suddenly see the earth from such an angle, the smoke above the lines and the spray of impacting shells. The altimeter indicates only 400 metres, and a rather uncomfortable jolt beneath the wings warns that one has just flown through the path of a very recently fired shell. A lack of fuel and ammunition call for a return home to the airfield.

'While flying back, new large enemy formations are discovered at the front. Not far from the airfield the aircraft flying home also encounter the birds with the yellow noses, Jagdstaffel 27.

'A day of great battle! The enemy has assembled an incredible number of fliers here. But Jagdgeschwader III will make it. After landing, there is a short critique and discussion by the commander. The mechanics get the aircraft ready

On 3 September Hermann Frommherz continued his meteoric scoring run by shooting down two RE 8s from No 12 Sqn. Frommherz is pictured in his quarters in Aniche – decorating the wall is the rudder fabric and fuselage roundel from Bristol F 2B Fighter E2514, which he had shot down on 27 August. Higher up, the black griffin emblem of SPA83 is glimpsed, cut from MdL Conraux's SPAD XIII No 8262, captured on 24 July. Well-known photos of Oswald Boelcke and Frommherz' friend Werner Voss are seen on the table and the shelf (courtesy of B Schmäling)

again. And it starts all over again. The pilots return home in ever greater triumph. This is a day on which victory is heaped upon victory. The thick swarms of English aircraft are scattered. Whoever was not forced to the ground crawled home with crippled wings or dove away at full revs. The air defence officers, who beforehand were so terribly agitated over the excessive amount of enemy aerial activity, report the same thing. But on the ground a tremendous battle continues. Indeed, the front has been relieved by the despatching of the enemy aerial forces, but one can hardly stand up to the pressure on the ground.'

Brzenk continued, telling of the afternoon attacks on ground targets, including British tanks and motorised reserve columns. All the *Staffeln* returned safely, and he concluded;

'In the meantime the reports from the front have arrived. The telephone is constantly in use. The *Geschwader* adjutant, Oblt Dahlmann, himself half deaf and dazed by the day's strenuous flying, reports "26 enemy aircraft have been shot down in the course of the day and lie on our side of the front [sic]. The *Geschwader* has no losses".'

SUCCESS CONTINUES

Loerzer's airmen had no opportunity to rest on their laurels, as the intense level of combat continued for several days. On 3 September, no less than ten more victories came to the *Geschwader* in exchange for one pilot killed. Early in the morning *Jasta* 36 was attacked by SE 5as from No 56 Sqn. Hübner was credited with one of them for his third, and Vzfw Skworz latched onto the tail of 1Lt A Vickers' SE 5a. Vickers was killed in the combat (falling to Skworz or Hübner or both), but then Canadian Capt W Irwin shot down Skworz in flames. The *Jasta* 36 diary states that both Skworz and his victim fell near the railway station at Saucourt – sadly, Skworz' watch, boots, and money were looted by German soldiers, indicative of the desperate state of the ground forces at this time.

At 1125 hrs Theodor Quandt shot down an SE 5a from No 60 Sqn. Next, Otto Löffler claimed a DH 9 at 1625 hrs, and at 1740 hrs Loerzer and *Jasta* 26 engaged the SE 5as of No 32 Sqn, with Loerzer shooting down one five minutes after Fruhner claimed a 'Camel' (sic) at Sin le Noble.

About 25 minutes later, both Quandt and Lindenberger recorded Bristols downed. *Jasta* 27's proficient CO Frommherz added two RE 8s to his own victory log, but the first one was, again, counter-claimed by Noltenius. He wrote that they took off at 1100 hrs and then, 'Frommherz dived on a two-seater. Because of my particular diving technique I was there earlier and had a better position for the attack by catching him head-on and positioning myself below him in a 180-degree turn. Then I pulled up, fired, and he was a goner. Presumably Frommherz fired at the very same moment. Because he claimed the kill

On 4 September the Fokker aces of *Jasta* 26 mauled a formation of Camels from No 70 Sqn, with Loerzer, Dahlmann, Fruhner and Buder all taking part. This BMW-engined D VII bearing the black/white markings of *Staffel* 26 is seen after it had been turned over to the British following the armistice. It was photographed on Serny airfield in January 1919 by American ace Bogart Rogers of No 32 Sqn

for himself, I had to waive it'. Noltenius was growing ever more disgruntled about his denied claims.

On 4 September Bolle of *Jasta* 'B' went on leave and Löffler was named acting CO. The *Geschwader* maintained its incredible scoring run for the third consecutive day, with 15 more victories. In the morning *Jastas* 26 and 27 bounced the DH 4s of No 18 Sqn as they were returning from a raid on Aubigny-au-Bac. Frommherz shot one down in flames. Noltenius attacked another, but then, he wrote, 'I came into his observer's well-aimed machine gun fire. He put bullets through the upper wing, a cabane strut and the elevator. To top it off, I got a grazing shot in the helmet'. Noltenius broke off and returned to his *Staffel,* and soon 'A lively aerial battle with a strong Sopwith squadron commenced'. The Sopwiths were 12 Camels (two flights) from No 70 Sqn, and once again Loerzer's Fokker pilots would decimate a squadron of Clerget-engined Camels.

When this onslaught was over, Oblt Dahlmann had added two more to his score, *Jasta* 26's deadly duo of Fruhner and Buder each got three and Loerzer and Ltn d R Ehlers tallied one apiece – as did *Jasta* 27's Lux – for a total of 11 victories. Although they had over-claimed by three, No 70 Sqn nevertheless had three pilots killed and five taken prisoner. Once again, Noltenius filed a counter-claim against Lux for one of the Camels – D3406, flown by 2Lt W M Herriott, who became a PoW. In spite of the fact that it was awarded to Lux, Noltenius acquired the rudder fabric from this Camel and kept it for many years.

Also on the 4th, *Jasta* 'B's' Bormann shot down an SE 5a, as did two *Jasta* 36 pilots – Quandt and Hübner. Kurt Jentsch of *Jasta* 'B' was badly wounded in his left leg, but instead of taking to his parachute he chose to make the 20-minute flight back to Emerchicourt, where he landed safely. When his mechanics lifted him

Paul Bäumer scans the skies for enemy aircraft on the *Staffel* airfield. Note the *Jasta* 'B' Fokker in the background. He returned to the front in early September and rapidly made up for lost time, recording 16 victories that month

out of the cockpit, Jentsch discovered that his parachute had been shredded by bullets. *Jasta* 36 lost Ltn Waldheim and Uffz Neumann – the latter pilot was severely wounded in the stomach and arm, and although he too managed to fly back to his airfield, Neumann died in hospital. However, this day also saw the welcome return of Paul Bäumer to *Jasta* 'B', fully recovered from his crash injuries.

The loss of three pilots in two days, an apparent lack of suitable fighter aircraft and the rationing of fuel now combined to reduce the combat readiness of *Jasta* 36. The unit would not record another victory (or casualty) until 4 October.

In the late afternoon of 5 September, a vee-formation of five Camels from No 4 Sqn of the Australian Flying Corps was patrolling over Douai. The formation, at 4250 metres, was led by Lt N C Trescowthick. 1Lt Len Taplin DFC, an old hand with 12 victories, was flying at the rear, and he had nervously climbed another 300 metres above the four Camels ahead of him when the flight was jumped by *Jastas* 26 and 27. Taplin subsequently wrote;

'There were three formations of enemy machines, all Fokker biplanes. Two formations of about 12 to 15 machines attacked almost simultaneously, one from high up in the west and one from the north. Later, a very much larger formation came in from the east.

'Trescowthick dived away under the formation coming from the direction of our own lines, but the others were cut off. I was gaining all the height I could, and as the formation from the north closed in, I dived into the middle of them. The leader pulled up and we went at it head-on. I got a good burst into his radiator and he went down in a glide. Next moment I was right in the middle of them, and before I could do anything a German below pulled his nose up and put a burst right through the bottom of my machine. One bullet went through my right hand, smashing it up and breaking my wrist.

'I was getting shot about, and firing at anything I saw, when a Fokker from somewhere (the sky seemed full of them) again got a burst into me. One bullet, an explosive, smashed the breech and crank-handle of one of my guns and sent a splinter through my nose. This dazed me and I fell out of control in an engine-spin. I spun down to about 1000 ft and then recovered, only to find two Fokkers had followed me down. I was down to about 100 ft and started off toward home. After running the gauntlet of ground fire for several miles, I was shot down when within a few hundred yards of the German frontlines.'

Taplin was captured, credited to Mesch of *Jasta* 26. He was luckier than three of his comrades who were killed – they were claimed by Frommherz, Lux and Classen.

The report by the *Kofl* of the 17th Army for the week of 11-18 September 1918 listed the victories amassed by each of the *Staffeln* in JG III in the period from 18 February to 5 September 1918. These totals were as follows – *Jasta* 'Boelcke', 77; *Jasta* 26, 94; *Jasta* 27, 50; *Jasta* 36, 29 victories for a cumulative total of 250 in 202 days of combat.

As September went on, so did the grim statistics. In the late morning of the 6th, *Jasta* 'B's' Bäumer and Löffler removed F 2Bs from No 11 Sqn's inventory, and later Lindenberger and Bormann both claimed Camels. On that day Noltenius wrote of his 4 September victory claim, 'As I had learned in the evening that the "victory-in-dispute" question had been settled without hearing me, I requested a revision of the decision. After a long talk, Loerzer said that I should hand in a report'. The next day he heard that the case was decided against him, and on the 8th he requested a transfer to another *Staffel.*

That transfer would come, but not before Noltenius made more contributions to the *Geschwader* epic. At 1730 hrs on 14 September he made his most famous balloon attack, which he reported in his diary;

'At an altitude of 3000 metres I flew toward the Front. And then, with the engine throttled back, flew deeper and deeper into enemy territory until I was in a position behind the balloons. At the Arras-Cambrai road, near Vis-en-Artois, I clearly saw the yellow balloon. As thin veils of clouds passed below me, I started my dive. I pulled in the direction, and in front of, the balloon until I was a bit lower and then pulled up to lose speed (if the prop revved too fast, there was a danger of the bullets hitting the airscrew).

'As soon as I was on the same level with the balloon, I applied full throttle and headed toward it. At a distance of 300 metres I began to fire, closing in and firing continuously. I only wanted to press the attack home, when suddenly, while I was a mere 50 metres away, a gigantic flame rose that completely engulfed me! The shock hurled me away. I at once took course for the lines after I had discovered that the machine was still in flying condition. But what a shambles she was! The cloth covering had become completely slack all over the machine and it billowed. Large shreds of balloon cloth hung in the struts and in the empennage. The controls acted perfectly differently. Fortunately, the strong western wind carried me home to our lines and I was able to land safely on our field (seventh confirmed victory).'

Noltenius was convinced that the British had attempted to trap him by detonating charges from the ground to explode the balloon (as had been done to the famous Rudolph von Eschwege in the Balkans). In later years, Noltenius wrote a second account of this incident in which he elaborated on the damage to his D VII;

'The metal sheets of the engine cowling were bashed in, the propeller charred, my beautiful painted insignia blown off by the explosion, the fabric covering brittle like tinder and torn loose in many places. Even my leather cap had been singed. But the explosion had been so brief that

Jasta 36 retained some triplanes long after the rest of JG III. This well-worn and heavily over-painted *Staffel* 36 Dr I was photographed at least as late as 19 August, since the other aircraft partially visible are Fokker E Vs. The ultimate form of *Balkenkreuz* has been painted in the specified extreme outboard positions. On 17 September a British bombing raid destroyed three *Jasta* 36 Fokkers (a Dr I, a D VII and an E V), leaving the *Staffel* with only one serviceable aeroplane

Here is the result of Friedrich Noltenius' exploit of 14 September, when he flew his D VII through the explosion of the 5th KBS (SR135) balloon. Noltenius had hoped to destroy three British gasbags that afternoon, but his first intended victim had been packed with explosives that were detonated from the ground. Noltenius wrote, 'There was no resistance to the controls, and there were big pieces of fabric everywhere in the struts. What had become of my youthful Fokker? – a tired, asthmatic old man covered with ulcers. I slowly took a course toward home at half-throttle. Only one flak battery boomed away, but it fired on a false psychological precept. It calculated my turns in advance and hurled its shells first to the right, then to the left. Of course, it did not occur to them that I was not at all capable of turning'

I myself had not felt the heat at all. The single gain was large shreds of the English balloon that were hanging about on the struts and tail. It was good rubberised fabric, but unfortunately not enough to make a raincoat.'

Noltenius would fly Sgt Willy Kahle's D VII as a replacement for a few days.

During the busy evening of the 15th, *Jasta* 26 aces Riemer and Mesch both crashed SE 5as, with the latter also adding a British balloon to his tally. Noltenius and Neuenhofen attacked some two-seaters, and Noltenius was 'viciously shot' at by one of the gunners – a tracer bullet hit a steel attachment plate for the centre section strut in his top wing, after which the spent round hit his chest directly above his heart. Noltenius' jacket was pierced and scorched and he received minor burns, but he was still credited with a victory. His fellow *Jasta* 27 pilot Ernst de Ritter was not as lucky, for after downing an SE 5a for his sole victory, he was shot in the side and wound up in a field hospital.

Jasta 26 was back in action on the 16th when Bristol F 2B Fighters from No 11 Sqn fell to the lethally consistent Fruhner and Lang – Christian Mesch and Ltn Marcard also recorded victories in the evening. *Jasta* 'B's' Löffler claimed two more Bristols and his *Staffel* comrade Bäumer destroyed another in flames. However, if this was the combat that Bäumer later wrote about (but did not date), he was attacked by 'an Englishman hanging on my tail' just as he was shooting up the two-seater. His cockpit was enveloped in flames and Bäumer took to his parachute. As he was descending he had to rid himself of one of his fur boots that was on fire through 'the most frantic contortions. That was aerial acrobatics in the truest sense of the word'. He landed safely just behind the German trenches.

On 17 September, wrote Noltenius, 'When I awoke in the morning I heard the noise of engines, flak fire and the high whine of the English machines'. Camels from No 209 Sqn and SE 5as from No 64 Sqn were paying a visit to the airfield at Aniche, dropping 91 bombs and strafing hangars and huts. Noltenius observed dismissively;

'They achieved practically nothing. Of the three operative *Staffeln,* none got damaged. Only a tent of *Jasta* 36 was set aflame while another one was virtually riddled with bullets. Three aeroplanes burned – a triplane, a parasol (E V) and a D VII.'

After his previous D VII was written off on 14 September, Noltenius eventually received a replacement, D VII (Alb) 5278/18. It was marked with the *Jasta* 27 yellow nose, and Noltenius had the full, ornate style of the Bremen flag applied to the fuselage and the centre section of the top wing. It was named *HERTHA* in honour of Noltenius' sister. This is an early view of the machine in pristine condition – there is evidence that *Jasta* 27 dispensed with the yellow tail marking to some extent by the war's final weeks

Noltenius' comment about the three *operative* squadrons is interesting, as it indicates that *Jasta* 36 had been out of action in recent days due to a lack of aircraft. Indeed, the *Jasta* 36 war diary confirms the destruction of the three aeroplanes, adding that the unit had only *one* usable aircraft left.

20 September 1918 was another day of intense combat for JG III that resulted in the unit losing the services of one of its most consistent performers. In the early morning *Jasta* 27 clashed with SE 5as of No 60 Sqn and Camels from No 201 Sqn. Frommherz, Noltenius and Neuenhofen all put in successful claims for fighters downed. At 1445 hrs, Camel pilots of the USAS's 148th Aero Squadron met JG III again. Noltenius reported that, after he watched Klimke chase one Sopwith down into the clouds, he 'saw another Sopwith coming in our direction, planning to catch Klimke from the rear. I attacked him head-on and shot well from this position. Thereupon, he turned away, but not tightly enough. I positioned myself behind him and, after aiming carefully, fired. Although the distance between us was nearly 40 metres, the aeroplane burst into flames after a short burst'.

Noltenius' D VII (Alb) *HERTHA* remained at *Jasta* 27 after he left the unit, and a number of photos show it in British possession at Nivelles after the war. By this time the tail section had been overpainted in perhaps an off-white or very pale yellow colour. The rudder is a replacement item from a different D VII

A different view of D VII (Alb) 5278/18 at Nivelles provides a look at the personal marking carried on the top wing. One of Loerzer's D VIIs can just be seen in the hangar at right *(courtesy of the 1914-1918 Aviation Heritage Trust)*

The doomed Camel pilot was 1Lt H 'Jenk' Jenkinson, a close friend of Elliott White Springs, his flight commander. Springs wrote of Jenkinson, 'He was putting up a wonderful fight but there were too many of them. A lucky shot winged "Jenk" and he burst into flames not 30 yards from me'.

One hour later, *Jastas* 'B' and 26 were in a huge brawl with three RAF fighter units – Nos 85 (SE 5as), 87 (Dolphins) and 203 (Camels) Sqns. Bäumer, Brandt and Fruhner all came away with Camel victories, but Fruhner's came at a high price. He reported that his D VII collided with one of the Camels, forcing him to take to his parachute. In landing, he sustained injuries severe enough to require a lengthy recovery. There is also a suggestion that he was shot down by No 203 Sqn's 2Lt W H Coghill, who reported firing at a D VII and seeing its wings fold up and its pilot bailing out (2Lt W H Coghill should not be confused with Frommherz' victim of 25 July, Lt F S Coghill of No 43 Sqn!). Although he returned in early November, Fruhner would never add to his score of 27. During the evening of 20 September the *Jasta* 27 pilots celebrated their 100th victory.

Fruhner's departure was a loss JG III could ill afford, and another blow came the very next day. During the evening of the 21st, Bäumer was credited with three 'DH 9s'. One of these was a No 27 Sqn DH 4 that fell in flames. *Jasta* 27's Klimke seems to have attacked the same group of DH 4s just minutes after he had shot up a Camel (his 17th victory) from No 209 Sqn. However, as Noltenius wrote, 'Klimke had been wounded, but he had safely returned to the base. During an attack on two-seaters he had been hit in a mysterious manner. He was hit three times in the shoulder'. Klimke left for a field hospital and was placed in the same ward as Ernst de Ritter. Shortly thereafter Klimke received even more serious injuries when the hospital was bombed, but once more he cheated death.

On 22 September JG III met up with Camel pilots of the USAS's 17th Aero Squadron again, and the result was one of the best-documented fights of the war. In 1978 historian Jon Guttman pieced the accounts of the combat (from both sides) together. Noltenius wrote that, 'At 0700 hrs the entire *Geschwader* took off. We climbed to great altitude. It did not take long and soon enemy single-seaters appeared, coming from towards Albert'. The enemy scouts consisted of 'C' Flight of the 17th, with 'B' Flight – led by 1Lt George A Vaughn Jr – about 900 metres above and behind.

Vaughn sighted 15 Fokkers coming from the east on a parallel course – he watched them to see if they would dive on 'C' Flight. They did precisely that, although Noltenius had spotted 'B' Flight and flew directly in front of Vaughn in order to entice him to attack. Vaughn decided he needed to come to the aid of 'C' Flight and led his flight down in a vertical dive on the D VIIs, which he described as having yellow noses and tails. Vaughn recounted, 'I saw that I was on the tail of one Fokker so I let him have a burst until he fell of out of control'. The Fokker was in fact flown by Noltenius, who was not out of the fight but circled back as Vaughn targeted another Fokker.

'Then', wrote Noltenius, 'another Fokker wedged himself between the Sopwith and me and the dogfight continued. Alternately, Mesch Neuenhofen and I were behind him'. Vaughn's description matches that of Noltenius. 'They were in each other's way, all of them determined to take a pot shot at my little Camel'. As he was evading his pursuers, Vaughn fired at another D VII that crossed in front of him, and Lt Dixon of 'B' Flight stated he saw it fall. Finally, Noltenius had to pull out of the fight because the fabric of his top wing was ripping away and several wing ribs were broken. Although Neuenhofen would get credit for downing Vaughn's Camel, the USAS pilot managed to escape in his crippled Sopwith by using his emergency fuel tank. Vaughn would subsequently receive the DSC for this action.

Camel pilot Lt G Thomas was killed, possibly by Frommherz, while Lt T Tillinghast was brought down and captured. *Jasta* 26 pilots Riemer and Brandt, as well as Oblt Loerzer, were also awarded with Camel victories from this fight.

On 24 September Bäumer chalked up a DH 9 and a scout to bring his tally to 32, while Löffler destroyed a DH 9 from No 49 Sqn for his 12th. That same day, the *Jasta* 36 war diary reported that some D VIIs had finally reached the *Staffel*. On 25 September Noltenius would make his last contribution to JG III's record book by shooting down a Sopwith in flames for his 13th victory. His request for a transfer was finally approved, and on the 27th he left for JG I. In the 'Richthofen' *Geschwader* Noltenius would initially fly with *Jasta* 6 before joining *Jasta* 11, bringing his total to 22. Like Frommherz and Fruhner, he would be proposed for the *Pour le Mérite* but fail to receive it because of the armistice.

Paul Bäumer continued to score in spectacular fashion in late September 1918, achieving his third and fourth 'triples' on the 27th and 29th of the month. This photo was taken in his hometown of Duisberg to show his long-awaited *Pour le Mérite*, which was awarded on 2 November 1918. Among his medal ribbons is one for the Royal Hohenzollern House Order Knight's Cross with Swords, although there is no record of him having officially received it (*L Bronnenkant*)

CHAPTER FIVE

BITTER END

Oblt Kurt von Griesheim, having arrived at *Jasta* 'Boelcke' in August, achieved his first and only victory on 30 October by bringing down an SE 5a at Fresnes. D VII (F) 4348/18, marked with the Berlin coat-of-arms on the sides and top of the fuselage, may well have been flown by Griesheim. It is seen here post-armistice, as an RAF pilot prepares to try it out. Many Allied pilots were eager to test fly D VIIs after the war, and the colourfully marked BMW Fokkers of JG III drew a lot of attention

From late September 1918 to the end of the war, *Geschwader* operations were hampered by frequent changes of airfield and the rationing of fuel. On the 26th, the Camels of No 203 Sqn, Bristol F 2B Fighters of No 22 Sqn and SE 5as from No 40 Sqn attacked the neighbouring Lieu St Amand aerodrome. JG III intercepted the raiders and *Jasta* 'B's' Bormann earned his 11th victory by downing the Camel of 2Lt W H Coghill of No 203 Sqn – Coghill was the possible victor over Otto Fruhner six days earlier. In the weeks to come, due in part to the recent departures of Fruhner, Klimke and Noltenius, *Jasta* 'Boelcke' came to the fore and would score the lion's share of JG III's victories.

The Battle of the Canal du Nord opened on 27 September, with a direct assault on the German 17th Army Front. By the evening the British were across the Canal du Nord and advancing on Cambrai. Even as the *Geschwader* was evacuating and moving to Lieu St Amand, its pilots scored prolifically on a day of intense aerial action. *Jasta* 'B' added nine more victims to its log. Four of the victories attained on the 27th were recorded as an unknown type of English single-seater, with two falling to Bormann, one to Bäumer and another to newcomer Uffz Karl Fervers. These claims may reflect encounters with the new Sopwith Snipes of No 43 Sqn, which recorded combats but no losses. Additionally, Bäumer shot down the SE 5a of No 56 Sqn's Lt G Mackenzie (who was killed in action) and a DH bomber for another 'hat trick'. Vallendor claimed two

Camels behind the German lines, and another SE 5a (from No 32 Sqn?) fell to Bassenge – the SE was joyfully recorded in the *Jasta* 'Boelcke' claim book as the *Staffel's* 300th victory.

The spoils of the day were shared with *Jastas* 26 and 27, with Frommherz getting two SE 5as while Fritz Classen shot down a Bristol F 2B Fighter from No 88 Sqn and an SE to bring his score to ten. Overall, JG III had claimed 13 victories. However, *Jasta* 'B' lost Ltn Fritz Heinz, killed near Awoingt by No 56 Sqn pilots.

Jasta 'B' pilots tallied three kills on the 28th. In the morning, Bassenge shot down SE 5a B7900 from No 64 Sqn – its pilot, 2Lt A Sheldrake, was badly wounded and soon died in captivity. Karl Fervers claimed a Camel for his second victory in two days, while Löffler chalked up his 13th with an SE 5a behind the German lines.

29 September brought four more triumphs to *Jasta* 'B', but the unit lost Ltn Fritz Hoffmann, who fell in combat against SE 5as from No 64 Sqn. Around midday, Karl Fervers continued his impressive start by shooting down No 22 Sqn's Bristol F 2B E2517 east of Cambrai – Lt C W M Thompson, a 12-victory ace, was slightly wounded and taken prisoner, along with his observer, Lt L R James. Bäumer and Uffz Paul Keusen were each credited with shooting a Bristol down in flames (No 22 Sqn also lost a second F 2B that day, with 1Lt E Adams and Sgt G H Bissell being killed). The indefatigable Bäumer was additionally recorded as also downing a Camel southeast of Sailly and an SE 5a near Bourlon Forest to achieve his third 'triple' of September, and his fourth overall – this brought his total to 38. Carl Bolle wrote '[*Jasta* "Boelcke"] finished up [September] with a total of 46 victories, the highest monthly total in the entire time of its existence'.

Willy Kahle of *Jasta* 27 earned the last four of his six victories in ten days between 26 October and 4 November 1918. Before joining a Hussar regiment in 1911, he had been a professional motorcycle rider. After training at *Jastaschule* II, he had been posted to *Jasta* 27 on 29 July 1918 *(courtesy B Schmäling)*

The end of September again saw the *Geschwader* pulling up stakes and retreating. *Jasta* 'Boelcke' transferred to Spultier, while the other three *Staffeln* moved to Saultain, all in the southern vicinity of Valenciennnes. On 2 October Bruno Loerzer's successful leadership of JG III was recognised with a promotion to Hauptmann.

'October', Bolle recounted, 'was already being taken up by the commencement of the withdrawal and frequent changes of base. Because of this, activities and successes were restricted. In the air, the opponent was now powerfully superior in numbers, and thus the number of [*Jasta* "B's"] victories went down to 18 [in October]'. On the 1st of that month, Ltn d R Neuenhofen of *Jasta* 27 claimed his tenth victory.

Bäumer put in a successful claim for a Bristol downed at Rumilly at 1430 hrs on 3 October, although there are few plausible corresponding RAF losses. He followed this up with another 'Bristol' on the 4th (more likely a DH 4 from No 25 Sqn), which fell near the Cambrai railway station. Bäumer now had 40 confirmed victories, matching the great Oswald Boelcke and putting him in the topmost tier of living German aces. Also on the 4th, *Jasta* 36 *finally* obtained some new aircraft when it picked up Pfalz D XII fighters from *AFP* 17. Even so, the engines of these machines had been fouled by 'used oil' and were useless until they were cleaned, taking up valuable time. Little is known of the combat use of these D XIIs. However, during the final retreat on 8 November, eight D XIIs could not be flown out because of bad weather so they were burned – two others managed to flee, only for their pilots to crash when they landed.

Jasta 'B' was in action on 5 October, with Bassenge sending a Camel down west of Crevecoeur for his seventh (and final) victory, and the 314th for his *Staffel*. Three days later the Second Battle of Le Cateau opened, and Bäumer participated in the corresponding air fighting by downing a 'Camel' near Bantigny, while Fervers claimed another between Cambrai and Cagnoncles for his fourth, and last, victory. A new *Jasta* 27 pilot, Ltn Willisch, added one more claim for an unknown type but his luck was short-lived.

Early in the morning of the 9th, Bristols from No 22 Sqn were escorting DH bombers when the latter came under attack from German fighters over the Forêt de Mormal. This action gave Bäumer his 43rd, and final, victory when he downed Bristol F 2B Fighter E2256 at Preseau. The pilot, Canadian Capt L Campbell, and his observer, 2Lt W Hodgkinson, both perished. Later that day *Jasta* 'B' stalwarts Vallendor and Löffler attacked DH 9s of No 107 Sqn as they were bombing the railway station at Mons. Vallendor 'made ace' by bringing down DH 9 F5846 at Sebourg – its pilot, 2Lt C Houlgrave, was captured, while observer 2Lt W M Thompson was badly wounded and soon died. Löffler tallied his 14th opponent by accounting for DH 9 D1107 – its crew of 2Lts Webb and J H Thomson also died.

From 10 to 13 October the *Geschwader* resumed its transient ways, moving to Lens, some 12 kilometres northwest of Mons. Due to logistical difficulties involved in the move, and the crippling shortage of fuel, frontline flights were severely curtailed. No more victories were noted until 14 October. What few records are available note that unspecified types of enemy aeroplanes fell to *Jasta* 27's Neuenhofen for his 11th victory and to Stoltenhoff for his third on the 14th. Sgt Kahle of the same *Staffel* achieved his second with an SE 5a. *Jasta* 27's elation over these hard-won successes was dampened by the wounding of Ltn Willisch.

On 30 October Alfred Lindenberger of the 'Boelcke' *Staffel* shot down an SE 5a from No 32 Sqn and destroyed another from the same unit two days later for his 12th victory. This BMW-engined D VII (F) 5109/18 is believed to be one of Lindenberger's Fokkers (he also flew OAW-built 4453/18), and is seen here in British hands after the armistice. The *Balkenkreuz* emblems on the rudder and fuselage have been covered over with white paint

Paul Bäumer had already left the front on the 12th, for along with Hptm Loerzer, he was attending the third fighter competition at Adlershof. On 2 November 1918, Bäumer would *finally* be given his long-overdue *Pour le Mérite*. Back on 12 February, prior to his commission, he had been awarded Prussia's Golden Military Merit Cross (the highest Prussian award for NCOs). Bäumer would stay at Adlershof until the Armistice.

Back at the front, JG III's success rate stagnated due to the lack of fuel and the general chaos associated with the retreat. Indeed, the *Jasta 36* war diary stated ruefully that no patrols were possible between 11 and 26 October. No *Geschwader* victories or casualties were recorded from 14 to 25 October – on the 25th, the only event of note was the death of *Jasta* 26's Ltn Gerhard Wohlgemuth. The next day Sgt Willy Kahle of *Jasta* 27 achieved his third victory, but this was balanced by the death of another *Jasta* 26 pilot, Uffz Fritz Zogmann. On the 27th Willy Neuenhofen increased his score to 12. 28 October brought one final flurry of five kills for *Jasta* 27, with *Staffelführer* Frommherz claiming a Bristol and a Camel while Kahle and two other pilots also gained victories. In fact, 28 through 30 October saw some of the most intense aerial combats of the entire conflict, as the *Jagdstaffel* and *Kest* pilots threw everything they had against the Allied raids on their troops and rail centres. On the 29th, *Jasta* 'Boelcke's' Bormann and Ltn d R Paul Blunck each downed Camels.

30 October is generally acknowledged as being the heaviest day of aerial combat in the war, and the pilots of JG III showed they were still a potent force by recording ten victories. At 1020 hrs *Jasta* 'Boelcke' bounced a group of No 32 Sqn SE 5as that were escorting bombers. *Jasta* 'B's' Oblt Kurt von Griesheim shot down one of the RAF fighters for his only victory, while the veterans Lindenberger and Bormann also bested SE 5as. No 32 Sqn lost aces American Capt A A Callender (eight victories) and Britain Lt R W Farquhar (seven), both killed, along with 2Lt W Amory taken PoW. DH bombers were credited to Löffler (15th victory) and Ltn d R Schlack (first). Ltn d R Blunck shot down DH 9 F6055 from No 98 Sqn – its pilot, Lt TW Sleight, was lightly wounded, while observer Lt E Dyke was killed. *Jasta* 26 was also in action against the DH 9s, with Lange downing one for his eighth *Luftsieg*. *Jasta* 27 contributed one Dolphin to the day's harvest.

1 November saw recent history repeat itself, as once again No 32 Sqn suffered the attentions of *Jasta* 'B'. Bolle, Lindenberger and Vallendor each downed an SE 5a – No 32 Sqn lost two pilots killed and another returned with a badly shot up aircraft.

On 4 November the skies cleared for one last day of massive aerial fighting. It was the last gasp for JG III, and its last day of combat was an epic finale. At 1015 hrs southwest of Mons, *Jasta* 26 apparently fought with Bristols of No 62 Sqn. Lange claimed one, which would have been

Jasta 'Boelcke' commander Carl Bolle rounded out his World War 1 career with a flourish on the final day of combat for JG III on 4 November 1918. He scored four times to contribute to the *Geschwader* total of 13 victories in exchange for one pilot killed *(L Bronnenkant)*

his tenth victory, but was denied this claim even though No 62 Sqn lost two crews. Later in the day three more Bristols were lost, this time from No 48 Sqn. The surviving F 2B crews reported that their Fokker assailants had yellow noses, which ties this fight to five claims for Bristols by *Jasta* 27 – two each to Frommherz and Neuenhofen and one to Kahle for their final victories.

Carl Bolle later wrote that *Jasta* 'Boelcke' had been out on a morning flight at high altitude and had 'polished off an English long-range reconnaissance aircraft and two fighters'. The latter were almost certainly Sopwith Snipes from No 4 Sqn of the Australian Flying Corps – the Aussies lost two examples at about 1115 hrs, one reportedly to ground fire and another that was hit by flak and then brought down by seven Fokkers. These were most likely Bolle's two misidentified 'SE 5a' victories. In the afternoon, however, *Jasta* 'B' and the Snipe pilots clashed again, as the No 4 Sqn pilots were escorting some DH 9s on a bomb raid. Bolle led just four other pilots into an attack on the Snipes. He shot down two Snipes and Bormann destroyed another one. Uffz Keusen of Bolle's *Staffel* was credited with a 'Bristol' this day, but he was later shot down (probably by one of the Snipe pilots) and killed.

On this fourth day of November, each of the four *Staffeln* of JG III contributed to the final day's tally of 13. At 1530 hrs, Erich Buder of *Jasta* 26 downed a DH 9 to top off his score at 12. Finally, *Jasta* 36 added its last victory when Ltn d R Otto Steger (who had scored once during his previous *Jasta* 53 service) brought down a Bristol at Tournai.

These were the last victories for JG III. Today, establishing a victory total for the *Geschwader* is a difficult task due to the destruction of many primary sources. What records that do survive are often contradictory. In fact, Friedrich Noltenius transcribed his diary for Luftwaffe archivists in 1936 because, as he stated, all JG III members had been asked to contribute any material 'because the war diary of the *Geschwader* was lost in the retreat'. No German historian or veteran ever published a history of the unit, unlike for JGs I and II. Based on the available data, however, we can make a conservative estimate that the pilots of *Jagdgeschwader Nr* III accumulated more than 370 victories in nine months of combat – a proud record that can stand against that of any other comparable unit.

In a sad postscript for the proud pilots of JG III, they were forced to hand over their Fokkers to the RAF after the war. One of the survivors was D VII (Alb) 5278/18, once flown by Noltenius. Here, it has been dismantled for transport by its new owners

APPENDICES

ACES WHO ACHIEVED VICTORIES SERVING WITH JG III

Jasta 'Boelcke'

Name	Total Victories
Ltn d R Paul Bäumer, PLM*	43
Oblt Carl Bolle, PLM	36
Ltn d R Hermann Frommherz	29/32
Ltn d R Ernst Bormann	16
Ltn d R Otto Löffler	15
Ltn d R Alfred Lindenberger	11
Ltn Karl Gallwitz	10
Ltn Gerhard Bassenge	7
Ltn d R Richard Plange	7
Ltn d R Hermann Vallendor	6

Jasta 26

Name	Total Victories
Hptm Bruno Loerzer, PLM	44
Vzfw Otto Fruhner	27
Vzfw Christian Mesch	13
Vzfw Erich Buder	12/13
Vzfw Otto Esswein	12
Ltn d R Fritz Loerzer	11
Vzfw Fritz Classen	10/11
Ltn d R Franz Brandt	10
Ltn Helmut Lange	8/9
Ltn d R Fritz Paul (Claus) Riemer	7/8
Oblt Theodor Hermann Dahlmann	7

Jasta 27

Name	Total Victories
Ltn d R Hermann Frommherz	29/32
Oblt Hermann Göring, PLM	22
Ltn d R Friedrich Noltenius	22
Ltn Rudolf Klimke	16
Ltn Wilhelm Neuenhofen	15
Offz Stv Willi Kampe	8
Vzfw Albert Lux	7/8
Sgt Willy Kahle	6

Jasta 36

Name	Total Victories
Ltn d R Heinrich Bongartz, PLM	33
Ltn d R Theodor Quandt	15
Ltn d R Hans Gottfried von Häbler	8
Ltn Kurt Jacob	7
Ltn d R Harry von Bülow-Bothkamp	6
Vzfw Alfred Hübner	6

* PLM indicates this pilot was officially awarded the *Pour le Mérite*. When two numbers are listed, that indicates there is a discrepancy between the total credited by most official sources and the number cited in *Jasta* war diaries or other sources, including the pilot himself

COLOUR PLATES

The art in this section was meticulously crafted by Harry Dempsey, who demonstrated immense patience working with the author to depict the aircraft as accurately as possible, given the available information. In selecting the photographs and the aeroplanes to be depicted in colour for this book, a conscious effort was made to avoid repeating illustrations that have appeared in previous Osprey publications. However, some duplication was unavoidable, and in two cases we have revised depictions presented in previous works based on new evidence. The colours depicted are approximations based on available data, as are the statements concerning location and dates. The author owes a huge debt to the research carried out by such authorities as Manfred Thiemeyer, Dave Roberts, Bruno Schmäling, Lance Bronnenkant, Ray Rimell, Reinhard Zankl, Reinhard Kastner and the late Alex Imrie. Any errors are solely the responsibility of the author.

1

Albatros D III 2049/16 of Ltn Hermann Göring, *Jasta* 26, Habsheim, April 1917

Göring first flew this D III in *Jasta* 26 on 24 February 1917, and he took it with him when he was given command of *Jasta* 27 in May – his last flight in it was on 16 July. All other depictions of this machine show it in its familiar *Jasta* 27 markings of a black fuselage with white nose and tail, but we have chosen to depict it as it first appeared in *Jasta* 26. At this time the familiar black/white banded fuselage markings were not yet employed, and pilots used a variety of coloured fuselage bands and (sometimes) numbers on the fuselage and below the wings as identification. We have provisionally

depicted the fuselage stripes as black/white – note the streamers, which probably denoted a *Kette* leader. The uppersurfaces of the wings and tail were camouflaged at the factory in dark olive green, light Brunswick green and a chestnut brown (Venetian Red), while the undersurfaces were pale blue. The rudder was clear-doped natural linen.

2

Albatros D III (serial and pilot unknown), *Jasta* 26, Iseghem, summer 1917

There are a number of photographs that seem to show that the famous black/white banded *Staffel* markings that became the hallmark of *Jasta* 26 were applied in stages. Several indicate that some D IIIs of the unit bore only black bands on the clear-varnished fuselage at first, as shown here. The black bands were also applied to the camouflaged tailplane, and the fin and rudder were painted black. The wings and tail surfaces were otherwise camouflaged, as described for the previous D III. It may be presumed that the alternating white bands were probably completed at a later date.

3
Albatros D III 2070/16 (pilot unknown), *Jasta* 26, Iseghem, summer 1917

This may have been one of the first *Jasta* 26 aircraft to bear the full display of black/white unit markings on the fuselage and horizontal tail surfaces. When photographed, the fin and rudder retained their factory finish. The wings were left in their three-colour factory camouflage finish as previously described.

4
Albatros D V 1072/17 of Ltn d R Johannes Wintrath, *Jasta* 'Boelcke', Varsenaere, September 1917

This illustration supersedes profile number 15 in Osprey's *Aviation Elite Units 26 – Jagdstaffel 2 'Boelcke'*. Recently, a better photograph of this aircraft surfaced, showing that – in addition to Wintrath's recorded personal emblem of blue, white and green fuselage bands – the entire fuselage forward of the white tail assembly was painted a very light colour which we have interpreted as pale blue. The uppersurfaces of both wings were additionally painted in this pale colour. The black spinner (absent on this aeroplane) and white tail assembly were hallmarks of *Jasta* 'B' aircraft at this time. Many readers will note the similarity to Hermann Frommherz' familiar light blue Albatros D III of the same unit. It is possible that Wintrath was indeed a member of a *Kette* led by Frommherz.

5
Albatros D V 1027/16 of Ltn Hermann Göring, *Jasta* 27, Iseghem, August 1917

Now leader of *Jasta* 27, Göring first flew this early-production D V on 31 May 1917 and alternated between it and D III 2049/16 until 3 July. It displayed his usual colour scheme of a black fuselage with a white tail section and nose. The cross on the rudder displayed a very narrow black edging against the all-white background, and the white border on the fuselage cross was rather thicker than normal. The wings were left in typical factory finish of olive green and mauve camouflage, with pale blue undersurfaces.

6
Albatros D V (pilot and serial number unknown), *Jasta* 27, Iseghem, August 1917

This D V illustrates what is believed to be standard marking practice within *Jasta* 27 during this period – fuselage and tail section in black, with individual pilots' numbers displayed on a white band aft of the cockpit. The wings retained their green and mauve camouflage. However, various line-up photographs taken around this same period show that sometimes fuselage bands of other colours, as well as differently coloured noses, were also employed. It is believed that after the acquisition of Fokker Dr I triplanes, a general change was made to yellow tails and noses – a precise start date for this switch over cannot be determined.

7
Albatros D V 1103/17 (pilot unknown), *Jasta* 26, Iseghem, summer 1917

This D V displayed full *Jasta* 26 unit black/white unit markings applied to the entire fuselage and tail section. The fin and rudder were painted black, but a small rectangle encasing the original serial number on the fin was left unpainted. On this D V the wheel covers and undercarriage struts seem white, while centre section struts were probably black, as was the personal 'W' emblem. The wings retained their factory-painted camouflage and a rack of flare cartridges was affixed next to the cockpit. The pilot is unknown, but if the 'W' was a personal initial, then Ltn Karl Wewer and Ltn d R Wittenhagen are both plausible identities.

8
Albatros D V 2242/17 (pilot unknown), *Jasta* 26, Abeele, October 1917

This D V displayed a personal emblem of a dark circle on the fuselage, which may have been black. As on most *Jasta* 26 D Vs, the serial number of this machine was not obscured but was retained in a small unpainted rectangle. The wings probably displayed a factory finish of green/mauve camouflage.

9
Albatros D V 4409/17 of Uffz Paul Bäumer, *Jasta* 'Boelcke', Varsenaere, September 1917

This illustration is an improved replacement for Profile 14 in Osprey Aviation Elite Units 26 *Jagdstaffel 2 'Boelcke'*. A newly available photograph has enabled a more detailed delineation of Bäumer's edelweiss emblem. One of Bäumer's combat reports from 20 September 1917 described this emblem as appearing on a black background with red stripe borders. This aircraft also featured the 'Boelcke' *Staffel* unit marking of a white tail, complete with the black border that was often added. The wings were most likely in camouflage of dark green/mauve.

10
Albatros D V 2329/17 (pilot unknown), *Jasta* 26, Abeele, October 1917

Besides displaying the characteristic black/white markings of *Jasta* 26, this D V was identified by the *Turnerkreuz*, the insignia of the *Deutsche Turnerschaft*, or German Gymnastics Association. The letter F repeated four times represents the group's motto – *frisch, fromm, frölich, frei* (vigorous, pious, cheerful, free). As originally designed in 1844, the emblem was in the Hessian colours of red and white, and we have depicted it thus – but black and white is also possible. The wings appear to have been covered in five-colour printed fabric.

11
Albatros D Va 5663/17 (pilot unknown), *Jasta* 26, Bavichove, November 1917

Neither the location nor the approximate date of the photograph of this machine is confirmed, but it provides a look at *Jasta* 26 Albatros D Va types. The unidentified pilot of this D Va used an 'X' as a personal marking, which seems to have been repeated on the light blue underside of the starboard lower wing (possibly both wings). Sadly, the serial number is not fully legible either, but it may have been 5663/17. Again, a rack of flare cartridges was fitted.

12
Albatros D Va 5602/17 of Oblt Bruno Loerzer, *Jasta* 26, Bavichove, November 1917
Details concerning the precise date and locale of the photographs of this machine are lacking, but they do show the D Va Loerzer flew as commander of *Staffel* 26 in late 1917/early 1918, and possibly in his first days as CO of JG III. The usual black/white bands were applied to the fuselage, but the fin and rudder were painted white. The crosses under the lower wing displayed white borders, and a lengthwise black stripe was painted on the undersides of the lower wings – no doubt to distinguish the *Staffelführer's* machine. Loerzer had a flare cartridge rack and Oigee sight fitted.

13
Fokker Dr I 157/17 of Ltn Paul Schröder, *Jasta* 'Boelcke', Marcke, February/March 1918
A recently discovered photograph reveals that Schröder was apparently the pilot of this highly decorated triplane. The fuselage was striped in two colours and similar décor was eventually added to the interplane struts, which we have provisionally depicted as black and white. By this time the former unit marking of an all-white tail assembly had been replaced by a half-black, half-white tail section. The rudders remained white, but in some cases were outlined in black. The engine cowlings were generally black with a white faceplate.

14
Fokker Dr I (pilot and serial unknown), *Jasta* 26, Marckebeeke, February 1918
Photographs of triplanes in full *Jasta* 26 livery, yet still displaying Iron Cross national insignia, are quite rare and this one is striking. This Dr I's regular pilot remains unknown, but it was marked with a personal emblem of a 'V' in black on the sides and top of the fuselage, and (apparently) in white on the top wing. The white crossfields on both top and bottom wings were reduced with solid olive-brown paint to produce the required five-centimetre white borders.

15
Fokker Dr I (pilot and serial unknown), *Jasta* 36, Kuerne, February 1918
This triplane displayed the blue engine cowling that identified *Staffel* 36 aircraft by this time, although the precise *shade* of blue remains a subject of argument – and may have changed from one period and aeroplane to another. Other hallmarks of most *Jasta* 36 triplanes were the auxiliary struts fitted to the landing gear axle fairing (in common with many *Jasta* 'B' Dr Is) and an access hole in the fuselage just aft of the cowling above the thrust line – covered with a circular panel. There is little doubt that this machine would also have borne a large Iron Cross insignia painted on the upper surface of the tailplane. This was an attempt to improve recognition of the triplane as a German machine when viewed from behind, and it became something of a *de facto* unit marking for *Jasta* 36 Dr Is. The pilot's personal emblem was the zigzag band stripe on a fuselage band.

16
Fokker Dr I 441/17 of Ltn d R Heinrich Bongartz, *Jasta* 36, Erchin, March 1918
On 30 March 1918 this Dr I suffered damage to the leading edge of its upper wing and the resultant loosening and tearing of the fabric on that wing. According to Alex Imrie, this damage may have occurred from a flak shell burst that also slightly wounded Bongartz, but the wound did not require him to leave the front. Dr I 441/17 bore the unit's blue engine cowling, the Iron Cross painted on the tailplane and the other *Jasta* 36 hallmarks previously discussed.

17
Fokker Dr I (serial unknown) of Ltn d R Hermann Frommherz, *Jasta* 'Boelcke', Halluin-Ost, May 1918
This Dr I is associated with Frommherz, as he was photographed posing in front of it, but that attribution remains tenuous. It displayed *Jasta* 'B' markings on the tail section, but when photographed it did not display the white faceplate on the black(?) cowling generally seen on triplanes of this unit. The 'diamond' markings on the fuselage and interplane struts are assumed to have been black/white. However, given Frommherz' associations with Lübeck, the Hanseatic colours of red and white are also slightly possible (although he was a Badener, Frommherz had served as an instructor in Lübeck and was awarded the Lübeck Hanseatic Cross). Later, as CO of *Jasta* 27, Frommherz flew a D VII marked with 'black and red vee stripes (chevrons) on the top wing', according to Ernst de Ritter. At his home long after the war, Frommherz possessed a D VII model that was *said* to replicate his markings. It had a yellow nose, and the top surfaces of both wings and the fuselage were basically black with red diagonal stripes. The yellow tailplane also bore two red chordwise stripes, and in that way displayed the Baden colours. Unfortunately, no photographs of his actual D VII have yet surfaced.

18
Fokker Dr I (pilot and serial unknown), *Jasta* 26, Halluin-Ost, May 1918
As seen in the classic shots taken by *Kogenluft* photographers in May, this Dr I displayed full *Jasta* 26 décor and a personal emblem of an 'X' on the fuselage. In *Jastas* 26 and 27, the pilots' personal emblems were often marked on the centre section of the top wing, as well as on the fuselage. We have opted to show the 'X' also painted on top of the fuselage on the white band adjacent to the national insignia, based on a close examination of the line-up photograph.

19
Fokker Dr I (pilot and serial unknown), *Jasta* 26, Halluin-Ost, May 1918
Another triplane from the official photographs was identified by a three-pointed 'Mercedes Star' painted on the fuselage as a personal emblem. This insignia was definitely repeated on the top wing centre section in white.

20
Fokker Dr I (pilot and serial unknown), *Jasta* 27, Halluin-Ost, May 1918
This machine bore the *Staffel* 27 hallmarks as described by Helmut Dilthey – yellow engine cowling, tail section and all struts. This particular machine retained a factory finish on its wheel covers when photographed, but some others from the unit had these components painted yellow. The unknown pilot's personal marking was a swastika on the fuselage, presumably in yellow – both views of this machine show that the leading arm of the swastika was considerably worn and degraded by the time the photographs were taken.

21
Fokker Dr I 577/17 of Ltn Rudolf Klimke, *Jasta* 27, Halluin-Ost, May 1918

This well-worn Dr I displayed Klimke's anchor marking, probably in yellow on the fuselage and in black on the uppersurface of the yellow tailplane. The circular access panel fitted just beneath the fuselage centre line aft of the cowling was a modification typical of triplanes of this *Staffel*. As noted, Klimke applied the anchor at his mother's insistence, as it symbolised good hope and she felt it would protect him from harm.

22
Fokker D VII (pilot and serial unknown), *Jasta* 26, Chambry, August 1918

A classic application of the unit's black/white markings was in effect on this Fokker-built D VII. The unidentified pilot's personal emblem was a '5' marked in black(?) on the fuselage and in white on the centre section of the top wing. The white paint forming the background for the '5' on the fuselage was rather thin and translucent in places.

23
Fokker D VII (serial unknown) of Ltn Rudolf Klimke, *Jasta* 27, Chambry, August 1918

Readers are advised that this depiction is quite provisional, being based on the poor and distant view of Klimke's D VII in the background of the photo of Klimke that formed the basis for Sanke postcard S674. The yellow nose was part of the standard *Jasta* 27 unit livery. There was a light-coloured band on the fuselage aft of the cockpit, which certainly *seems* to bear what looks like Klimke's anchor in black. The white borders of the vertical arm of the fuselage cross show up very distinctly (due to the optical effect of halation) and the tail was overpainted a light colour. We have tentatively chosen to interpret these markings as illustrated, with the tail being a rather lighter shade of yellow than the engine cowling. This D VII was probably covered in four-colour printed fabric, and bore two white-bordered black chevron-style stripes on the upper wing, clearly evident in the photograph.

24
Fokker D VII (F) (serial unknown) of Oblt Carl Bolle, *Jasta* 'Boelcke', Emerchicourt, September 1918

This is one of several D VIIs flown by Bolle in almost identical markings near the end of the war – the (F) suffix indicates a BMW-engined example. It displayed Bolle's usual fuselage bands in yellow – the colour of his *Kürassier-Regiment von Seydlitz (Magdeburgisches) Nr 7* – flanked by the black and white Prussian colours. It additionally had the remainder of the fuselage painted black, with the exception of the usual unit markings of the white nose and the black/white tail section. Bolle's D VIIs also sported two white chordwise stripes on the upper wing.

25
Fokker D VII (F) (pilot and serial unknown), *Jasta* 26, Lens, October 1918

Along with many other JG III fighters, this BMW-engined D VII was reluctantly delivered to the RAF at Nivelles soon after the armistice. It was fitted with the conical quick-release airscrew hub generally associated with BMW Fokkers. The personal marking was the 'Z' on the fuselage. The only known photos of this D VII were taken after the war when it was in British hands at Nivelles. The fin and rudder were

outlined in black, and they may have been replacement components from an Albatros-built D VII fitted to this Fokker-built machine. It is just possible this D VII was marked for Uffz Fritz Zogmann. If so, he was obviously flying a different aircraft when he was killed on 26 October 1918.

26
Fokker D VII (F) 5109/18 of Ltn Alfred Lindenberger, *Jasta* 'Boelcke', Lens, October 1918

Lindenberger also flew a different OAW-built D VII 4454/18 that had the diagonal striping applied to the fuselage from nose to tail, and was well documented in post-war photos. This BMW-engined D VII is also believed to have been flown by Lindenberger, as the fuselage markings are very similar to the other machine but somewhat abbreviated. The striping on the top of the fuselage angled aft, and it is thought that the stripes on the starboard side were angled in the reverse direction to those on the port side. The usual *Jasta* 'Boelcke' markings were seen on the nose and the black/white tail section, and the serial number was re-marked in small characters atop the rudder – a typical practice in this *Staffel*.

27
Fokker D VII (pilot and serial unknown), *Jasta* 36, Lens, October 1918

Confirmed photos of *Jasta* 36 D VIIs are scarce, but this Fokker-built machine was almost certainly from this *Staffel*. The application of the (presumably) blue *Staffel* marking on the nose was in exactly the same format and extent as the white display on *Jasta* 'Boelcke' Fokkers. It also bore a broad coloured band aft of the cockpit, and we have tentatively interpreted this personal marking to be the same blue as on the cowling. The remainder of the airframe was covered in four-colour printed fabric and had the finish typical of Fokker-built aircraft.

28
Fokker D VII (F) 4348/18 of Oblt Kurt von Griesheim(?), *Jasta* 'Boelcke', Lens, October 1918

This BMW-engined D VII (F) appears in several photos – some taken at *Jasta* 'B' at the very end of the war, and others taken after it had been turned over to the RAF at Nivelles. The crest on the fuselage displayed the famous 'Berlin Bear', leading the author and others to speculate that this D VII was the aircraft of Oblt Kurt von Griesheim – he was the only Berliner in the unit at war's end aside from Carl Bolle. Along with the usual *Jasta* 'Boelcke' markings on the tail and nose, it bore a typical finish of four-colour fabric on all surfaces. The metal cowling panels aft of the white nose marking appear quite dark, and *may* had been painted black as part of the *Staffel* livery, although we have chosen to leave them as factory finish dark green. The serial number was re-marked at the top of the rudder.

29
Fokker D VII (serial unknown) of Hptm Bruno Loerzer, JG III, Lens, October 1918

As *Geschwader* commander, Loerzer had at least two D VIIs (or three) that were finished similarly. The black and white stripes of *Jasta* 26 were extended to the uppersurface of the top wing and to the undersurface of the bottom wing to identify the commander's machine from all angles and to facilitate the leadership of large formations. The unpainted wing areas remained in the factory finish of five-colour fabric. Details include a tube for a flare pistol extending from the port side of the cockpit and an Oigee sight fitted between the guns. Finally, leader's streamers trailed from both interplane struts.

30
Fokker D VII (Alb) 5278/18 of Ltn d R Friedrich Noltenius, *Jasta* 27, Aniche, September 1918

This machine was flown by Noltenius after his OAW-built D VII was damaged in the balloon attack of 14 September. It was named *HERTHA* in honour of his sister, and displayed the usual *Jasta* 27 yellow on its nose and (apparently) wheel covers. The ornate red and white markings on the fuselage and centre section of the top wing were inspired by the flag of his birthplace, the free Hanse city of Bremen. One photo taken before war's end shows this D VII in these markings, but with the tail left in factory finish – it may have been flown in that guise by Noltenius for some time. When he transferred to *Jasta* 6 in late September, this D VII remained at *Jasta* 27 and was flown by other pilots. Several other photos show it after the fighter was turned over to the British at Nivelles. By then it had been painted a very light colour on the tail, and had also acquired a replacement rudder from a different D VII. While the light-coloured tail section could well have been off-white, we have chosen to provisionally portray it as a very pale yellow. Although this does not match the yellow on the nose, it is possible it was belatedly added as part of the display of *Jasta* 27 unit colours.

31
Fokker E V (pilot and serial unknown), *Jasta* 36, Chambry, August 1918

The photos of this *Jasta* 36 Fokker show the cowling appearing as a very light shade, which we have chosen to interpret as a lighter shade of the usual *Staffel* blue colour. Inconsistencies in pigments and shades of available blue paint are certainly probable under wartime conditions, and a lighter shade of blue would appear quite pale on the orthochromatic film of the day, especially in bright sunlight. The pilot's personal emblem was the star on the dark-bordered fuselage band, which we have provisionally illustrated as red. The remainder of the aircraft was covered in four-colour fabric, and the wing was finished in a streaky application of various camouflage colours.

32
Fokker D VII (F) 4361/18 (pilot unknown), *Jasta* 'Boelcke', Lens, October 1918

Unfortunately, no details are available concerning the pilot of this beautiful BMW-engined Fokker, nor of the date or location of the solitary photo. However, it displayed classic *Jasta* 'Boelcke' markings on nose and tail, and once again the serial number was repainted in small characters at the top of the rudder. The unknown pilot may (like Noltenius of *Jasta* 27) have hailed from Bremen, as the fuselage stripes certainly seem to indicate – we have thus depicted these markings as red and white. These personal colours were extended to the interplane struts and the wheel covers, but the centre section struts were only white. Four-colour fabric covered the airframe.

BIBLIOGRAPHY

Bailey, Frank and Cony Christophe, *The French Air Service War Chronology 1914-1918,* London, 2001

Bolle, C, *Jagdstaffel Boelcke (30. August 1916 – 24. November 1918)', In der Luft Unbesiegt,* G P Neumann, ed., Munich, 1923

Bolle, C, *Jagdstaffel Boelcke, Unsere Luftstreitkräfte,* W von Eberhardt, ed., Berlin, 1930

Bronnenkant, L, Ph D, *The Imperial German Eagles in World War I, Volume 1 and Volume 2,* Atglen, PA, 2006 and 2008

Brzenk, H, *Im Kampf gegen Kokarde und weissen Adler,* Berlin-Lichterfelde, 1925

Brzenk, Hans, (ed.), *Wir jagten den Feind,* Berlin, 1939

Cony, C and Martin, P, 'Au combat durant deux guerres mondiales, l'as Harry von Bülow-Bothkamp', *Avions,* No 59, Fevrier 1998

Ferko, A E, 'Jagdflieger Friedrich Noltenius, 1894 – 1936', *Cross & Cockade Journal,* Vol 7 No 4, 1966

Frank, N, *Jasta Boelcke, The History of Jasta 2, 1916-1918,* London, 2004

Franks, N, Bailey, F and Guest, R, *Above the Lines,* London, 1993

Franks, N, Bailey, F and Duiven, R, *The Jasta Pilots,* London, 1996

Franks, N, Bailey, F and Duiven, R, *The Jasta War Chronology,* London, 1998

Franks, N, Guest, G and Bailey, F, *Bloody April . . . Black September,* London, 1995

Franks, N and VanWyngarden, G, *Osprey Aircraft of the Aces 40 – Fokker Dr I Aces of World War 1,* Botley, Oxford, 2001

Franks, N and VanWyngarden, G, *Osprey Aircraft of the Aces 53 – Fokker D VII Aces of World War 1, Part 1,* Botley, Oxford, 2003

Gastreich, S and Waiss, W, *Aus dem Boelcke-Archiv: Jagdstaffel Boelcke, Band VIII 1914-1918,* Aachen, 2014

Grosz, P M, 'The Agile and Aggressive Albatros', *Air Enthusiast No 1,* 1976

Guttman, J, *Osprey Aviation Elite Units 28 – USAS 1st Pursuit Group,* Botley, Oxford, 2008

Guttman, J, *Osprey Duel 17 – SPAD XIII vs Fokker D VII, Western Front 1918,* Botley, Oxford, 2009

Hall, J N and Nordhoff, C B, ed., *The Lafayette Flying Corps, Volume I and II,* Boston and New York, 1920

Hamady, Theodore, *The Nieuport 28, America's First Fighter,* Atglen, PA, 2008

Henshaw, T, *The Sky Their Battlefield II – Updated, Expanded,* London, 2014

Imrie, A, 'D.VII, Sidelights on Fokker's Great Fighter', *Aircraft Illustrated Extra,* No 7

Imrie, A, 'Fokker Warpaint', *Flying Scale Models,* February 2004

Imrie, A, *Osprey Airwar 13 – German Fighter Units 1914-May 1917,* London, 1978

Imrie, A, *Osprey Airwar 17 – German Fighter Units June 1917-1918,* London, 1978

Imrie, A, 'Paul Bäumer – Iron Eagle', *Cross & Cockade Journal,* Vol 5 No 4, 1964

Imrie, A, *Pictorial History of the German Army Air Service,* London, 1971

Imrie, A, *The Fokker Triplane,* London, 1992

Imrie, A, *Vintage Warbirds 16: German Army Air Aces of World War One,* Poole, 1987

Jentsch, K, *Jagdflieger im Feuer, Kriegserlebnisse eines Kampf- und Jagdfliegers bein Jagdgeschwaderlll, Jagdstaffel Boelcke u.a.,* Magdeburg, 1937

Kilduff, Peter, *Hermann Göring, Fighter Ace,* London 2010

Lawson, S T, 'Royal Prussian Jagdstaffel Nr 36', *Cross & Cockade International Journal,* Vol 20 No 1, 1989

Levandowski, Ben, 'Jasta 26 During "Operation Michael"', *Cross & Cockade Journal,* Vol 16 No 4, Winter 1975

O'Connor, N, *Aviation Awards of Imperial Germany in World War I and the Men Who Earned Them,* Vols I to VII, Princeton, NJ, and Atglen, PA, 1988 to 2003

Olynyk, F J, 'The Combat Records of Hermann Göring', *Over the Front,* Vol 10 No 3, 1995

O'Neal, Michael, 'Lt Zenos R Miller, 17th Aero, USAS'. *Over the Front,* Volume 11, No 3, Autumn 1996

Puglisi, W R and Miller, T G, 'Jasta B', *Cross & Cockade Journal,* Vol 9 No 4, Winter 1968

Reed, O and Roland, G, *The Camel Drivers; The 17th Aero Squadron in World War I,* Atglen, PA, 1996

Revell, A, *British Single-Seater Fighter Squadrons on the Western Front in World War I,* Atglen, PA, 2006

Revell, A, *Osprey Aviation Elite Units 33 – No 56 Sqn RAF/RFC,* Botley, Oxford, 2009

Rimell, R (ed.), *Fokker D VII Anthology No 1,* Berkhamsted, 1997

Schäffer, Ernst, *Pour le Mérite, Flieger im Feuer,* Berlin, 1931

Taylor, S K, 'Surrogate Son – 2Lt Robert Howell "Bob" Cowan, C Flight, 65 Squadron, RFC 1917', *Over the Front,* Vol 24 No 2, 2009

Todd, Robert M, *Sopwith Camel Fighter Ace,* Falls Church, VA, 1978

VanWyngarden, G, *Osprey Aviation Elite Units 26 – Jagdstaffel 2 'Boelcke',* 2007

Vaughn, D (ed.), *Letters from a War Bird; The World War I Correspondence of Elliott White Springs,* Columbia, SC, 2012

Woolley, C, *First to the Front, The Aerial Adventures of 1st Lt Waldo Heinrichs and the 95th Aero Squadron,* Atglen, PA, 1999

Zuerl, W, *Pour le Mérite-Flieger,* Munich, 1938

Websites Consulted

www.buddecke.de
www.frontflieger.de
www.theaerodrome.com
www.overthefront.com

INDEX

References to images are in **bold**; references to plate captions are in brackets.